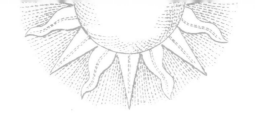

THE GREAT
HISPANIC HERITAGE

Ernesto "Che" Guevara

THE GREAT HISPANIC HERITAGE

THE GREAT
HISPANIC HERITAGE

Ernesto
"Che" Guevara

Dennis Abrams

CHELSEA HOUSE
PUBLISHERS
An imprint of Infobase Publishing

Ernesto "Che" Guevara

Copyright © 2010 by Infobase Publishing

Chelsea House
An imprint of Infobase Publishing
132 West 31st Street
New York NY 10001

Library of Congress Cataloging-in-Publication Data
Abrams, Dennis, 1960–
  Ernesto "Che" Guevara / Dennis Abrams.
     p. cm. — (Great Hispanic heritage)
  Includes bibliographical references and index.
  ISBN 978-1-60413-732-3 (hardcover : alk. paper) 1. Guevara, Ernesto, 1928–
1967—Juvenile literature. 2. Revolutionaries—Latin America—Biography—Juvenile
literature. 3. Guerrillas—Latin America—Biography—Juvenile literature. 4. Latin
America—History—1948–1980—Juvenile literature. 5. Cuba—History—Revolution,
1959—Juvenile literature. 6. Cuba—History—1959–1990—Juvenile literature.
7. Argentina—Biography—Juvenile literature. I. Title. II. Series.
  F2849.22.G85A624 2010
  972.9106'4092—dc22
  [B]   2010007514

Text design by Terry Mallon
Cover design by Terry Mallon/Keith Trego
Composition by EJB Publishing Services
Cover printed by Bang Printing, Brainerd, MN
Book printed and bound by Bang Printing, Brainerd, MN
Date printed: August 2010
Printed in the United States of America

10 9 8 7 6 5 4 3 2 1

Contents

The Man
on the T-shirt

On January 1, 1959, the army of Fidel Castro entered the city of Havana, Cuba, ending the seven-year dictatorship of Fulgencio Batista. A year and a half later, with Castro's government fully in control of Cuba and having officially declared itself communist, *Time* magazine placed on its cover one of Castro's chief allies in the revolution, Ernesto Guevara. It was probably the first time that much of the American public had heard his name. It would definitely not be the last.

Known as "Che" to his friends and troops, Guevara was one of three men who had led the revolution and were attempting to remake Cuba into a workers' paradise. *Time* magazine, concerned, as were many in America, about the danger of having a communist country just 90 miles (145 kilometers) from Florida, described the roles of Cuba's three most powerful men:

Prime Minister Castro, at 33, is the heart, soul, voice and bearded visage of present-day Cuba. His younger brother, Armed Forces Chief Raul Castro, 29, is the fist that holds the revolution's dagger. National Bank President Che Guevara, 32, is the brain. It is he who is most responsible for driving Cuba sharply left, away from the U.S. that he despises and into a volunteered alliance with Russia. He is the most fascinating, and the most dangerous, member of the triumvirate.

Wearing a smile of melancholy sweetness that many women find devastating, Che guides Cuba with icy calculation, vast competence, high intelligence, and a perceptive sense of humor.[1]

Just seven years later, Ernesto Guevara, now known throughout the world as "Che," was in Bolivia's Ñancahuazú valley. A trained doctor, writer, military leader, and revolutionary, Guevara had gone to Bolivia to help build an army to overthrow the military-supported government of President René Barrientos Ortuño. Che's army, just 50 strong, was known as the ELN (Ejército de Liberación Nacional de Bolivia; "National Liberation Army of Bolivia"). Although small, it was well equipped and had scored a number of impressive victories against Bolivian regular forces.

With his army seemingly unable to capture Guevara on its own, President Barrientos called on the United States for assistance. The United States, which had a history of supporting right-wing governments as a bulwark against communism, was only too happy to assist. Felix Rodriguez, a Cuban exile-turned-CIA Special Activities Division operative, was sent to Bolivia to lead the hunt.

On October 8, with the help of an informant's tip, Guevara's guerrilla encampment was surrounded by Bolivian Special Forces. Guevara was wounded in the attack and taken prisoner, shouting to his captors, "Do not shoot! I am Che Guevara and worth more to you alive than dead."[2]

Guevara was tied up and taken to a mud schoolhouse in the nearby village of La Higuera. He refused to answer the questions of his interrogators and would only speak quietly with low-ranking Bolivian soldiers. "He was a mess," wrote CIA agent Felix Rodriguez. "Hair matted, clothes ragged and torn."[3] In pain from his wounds, Guevara still managed to hold his head high, meeting his captors' gaze and asking only for something to smoke.

The next morning, October 9, Guevara asked if he could meet the *maestra*, the schoolteacher of the village, 22-year-old Julia Cortez. It has been reported that she found him to be an "agreeable looking man with a soft and ironic glance," but that she was "unable to look him in the eye," because his "gaze was unbearable, piercing, and so tranquil." During their brief conversation, Guevara complained to her about the condition of the schoolhouse, pointing out that it was wrong to expect poor students to be taught there while "government officials drive Mercedes cars," adding "that's what we're fighting against."[4]

Later that morning, Bolivian president René Barrientos gave the order that Guevara be killed. His executioner was Mario Terán, a sergeant in the Bolivian army who "won" the privilege by drawing the short straw after arguments broke out over which soldier would get the honor. To make the bullet wounds appear consistent with the story that the government planned to release to the public, Felix Rodriguez ordered Terán to aim carefully, in order to make it appear that Guevara had been killed in action, rather than simply killed in cold blood.

Moments before he was to be killed, Guevara was asked if he was thinking about his own immortality. "No," he replied. "I'm thinking about the immortality of the revolution." At which point Che Guevara, the man who had helped to lead the Cuban revolution, spat in the face of Bolivian rear admiral Horatio Ugarteche and told his executioner, "I know you've come to kill me. Shoot, coward, you are only going to kill a man."[5]

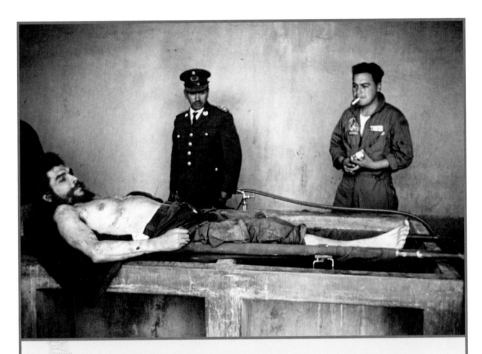

After his October 9, 1967, execution by the Bolivian government, Argentine revolutionary Ernesto "Che" Guevara's body was laid out and photographed for the world to see.

According to witnesses, Terán hesitated at first, and then opened fire with his semi-automatic rifle, repeatedly hitting Guevara in the arms and legs. Guevara writhed on the ground in pain, apparently biting one of his wrists to avoid crying out in front of his executioners. Terán then opened fire again, fatally wounding Guevara in the chest. In all, he was shot a total of nine times.

Guevara's corpse was then tied to the landing skids of a helicopter and taken to nearby Vallegrande, where photographs were taken for publicity purposes, showing his body lying on a bleak concrete slab in the laundry room of the Nuestra Señora de Malta hospital. It was important to the Bolivians to prove to the world that *they*, after years of effort by others, had been the ones to capture and kill the elusive Che. One of his captors, General Gary Prado Salmon, explained:

They washed, dressed and arranged him following instructions from the forensic physician . . . We had to prove his identity and show the world that we had defeated . . . Che. There was no question of displaying him the way other guerrillas were always exhibited, as corpses on the ground but with expressions that always had an enormous impact on me . . . their faces all twisted. That was one of the things that made me put the handkerchief on Che's jaw, precisely so it wouldn't be deformed. But what everyone wanted, instinctively, was to show that this was Che; to be able to say, "Here he is, we won.": this was the feeling among the armed forces of Bolivia.[6]

After the photos were taken and a military doctor had cut off Che's hands, Bolivian army officers sent Guevara's body to an undisclosed location, refusing to reveal whether his remains had been buried or cremated. His hands were preserved in formaldehyde and sent to Buenos Aires, where his fingerprints were on file with the Argentine police, to confirm that it was, indeed, Che. With that, the Bolivian government (along with many other right-wing governments around the world) hoped that Ernesto Guevara would be forgotten, just one more body on the ash heap of history, without a grave site to enshrine his memory.

It didn't turn out that way. His memory refused to die. No longer just a man, he had become a martyr to the cause of revolution and of the poor and oppressed; a man who had given his life to help improve the lives of others. Thirty-two years later, noted Chilean author and human rights activist Ariel Dorfman wrote about Che Guevara for *Time* magazine, which had named Che as one of the 100 most influential people of the twentieth century.

His execution in Vallegrande at the age of 39 only enhanced Guevara's mythical stature. That Christ-like figure laid out on a bed of death with his uncanny eyes almost about to open; those fearless last words . . . ; the anonymous burial and the hacked-off hands, as if his killers feared him more after he was dead than when he had been alive: all of it is scalded into the mind and memory of those defiant times. He would resurrect, young people shouted in the late '60s; I can remember fervently pro-claiming it in the streets of Santiago, Chile, while similar vows exploded across Latin America. ¡No lo vamos a olvidar! We won't let him be forgotten.[7]

Indeed, as Guevara's biographer Jon Lee Anderson points out in his biography *Che Guevara: A Revolutionary Life*, after his death,

> the Che myth grew and spiraled beyond anyone's control. Millions mourned his passing. Poets and philosophers wrote impassioned eulogies to him, musicians composed tributes, and painters rendered his portrait in a myriad of heroic poses. Marxist guerrillas in Asia, Africa, and Latin America anxious to "revolutionize" their societies held his banner aloft as they went into battle. And, as the youth in the United States and Western Europe rose up against the established order over the Vietnam War, racial prejudice, and social orthodoxy, Che's defiant visage became the ultimate icon of their fervent if largely futile revolt. Che's body might have vanished, but his spirit lived on; Che was nowhere and everywhere at once.[8]

With his death, he became a symbol of revolution, the image of change. The most famous photograph of Che, taken by fashion photographer Alberto Korda, became one of the best-known images of his time. As Jon Lee Anderson described it, "In it, Che appears as the ultimate revolutionary icon, his eyes staring boldly into the future, his expression a virile embodiment of outrage at social injustice."[9] But, as Paul Vallely pointed out in *The Independent*, the photograph soon became more than just a photo.

Soon the photograph became familiar all over the world. It soon spread from political circles to rock bands seeking to advertise their subversive credentials. But then the revolutionary became chic. Andy Warhol used it alongside images of Marilyn Monroe and James Dean in the iconography of pop art. By 1970 the defiant image had become, in the words of the British pop artist Peter Blake, "one of the great icons of the 20th century," appearing on posters, T-shirts, badges, and before long, appearing in utterly debased forms to advertise jeans, china mugs, canned beer, skis, holidays and even soap powder. Swatch released a watch with Che's image on its face. Madonna used it on a CD cover. Smirnoff slapped it on their vodka ads. (Korda sued over that.) The total inversion of everything Guevara stood for was a recent newspaper photograph

MARXISM

Marxism is a political philosophy and practice derived from the work of Friedrich Engels and Karl Marx. One of the most powerful and influential political movements of the early and mid-twentieth century, it has dropped in popularity as the flaws and difficulties in putting its theories into practice have become evident.

A basic tenet of Marxism is one of class struggle. On one side are the capitalists who own the means of producing the necessities of life. On the other side are the workers or proletariat who are forced to work for the capitalists in order to survive. According to Marx and Engels, the struggle between the two sides is the central element of all social change.

Marxism holds that such a system is exploitive as well as economically irrational. What it offers is an overthrow of capitalism to be replaced by a classless society in which goods are manufactured not because they are profitable, but because they are useful to society. These goods are not to be sold but showing Liz Hurley club-hopping across London in a Che T-shirt and clutching a $4,500 Louis Vuitton handbag.[10]

Indeed, to many, Che Guevara is not a real figure in history, but just a guy on a cool T-shirt. As Ariel Dorfman points out:

> This apotheosis of his image has been accompanied by a parallel disappearance of the real man, swallowed by the myth. Most of those who idolize the incendiary guerrilla with the star on his beret were born long after his demise and have only the sketchiest knowledge of his goals or his life. Gone is the generous Che who tended wounded enemy soldiers, gone is the vulnerable warrior who wanted to curtail his love of life lest it

instead are distributed according to the principal of (at first), "from each according to their ability; to each according to their work," and finally, in Marxism's most advanced stage "from each according to their ability; to each according to their needs."

In other words, under a Marxist system of government, a doctor, let's say, would no longer be working in order to earn large amounts of money. He would be working for society (let's call it the state) both because that is what he wants to do and because that is what the state needs. In return, he receives from the state the things that *he* needs. While this may sound good as an idealistic theory, to date, such a system has proved to be problematic to implement. It is perhaps possible that people are too driven to achieve personal success and achievement on their own to be willing to put it aside to create a society where there are no "winners" or "losers," but in which all are, in theory at least, "equal."

make him less effective in combat and gone also is the darker, more turbulent Che who signed orders to execute prisoners in Cuban jails without a fair trial.[11]

THE REVOLUTIONARY

To begin to understand Che Guevara, and why he was hated and loved by so many people worldwide, we have to begin by defining a couple of terms. Che Guevara was a revolutionary. According to the *Shorter Oxford English Dictionary*, a revolutionary is someone who "instigates or supports revolution; a participant in a particular revolution."[12]

And what, precisely, is a revolution? Here's how the *Shorter Oxford English Dictionary* defines it in general terms:

> The complete overthrow of an established government or social order by those previously subject to it; a forcible substitution of a new form of government.[13]

In other words, men as different as George Washington, Thomas Jefferson, Mao Zedong, and Ernesto Guevara were revolutionaries: people who fought to overthrow or replace the form of government under which they were living and substitute for it a new government—one, in theory at least, more responsive to the needs of the people.

To Americans, then, George Washington and Thomas Jefferson are heroes, the fathers of our country. To the British of that time, though, they were an enemy to be defeated: rebels who were using guerrilla warfare techniques to remove forcibly a legitimate government and replace it with one of their own invention. The case of Che Guevara is similar. Depending on which side you're on, Ernesto Guevara was either a heroic revolutionary or a terrorist. It is, as has been said, all a matter of perspective.

Not everybody sees the life of Che Guevara in a positive light. Writing for *Slate*, Paul Berman notes that:

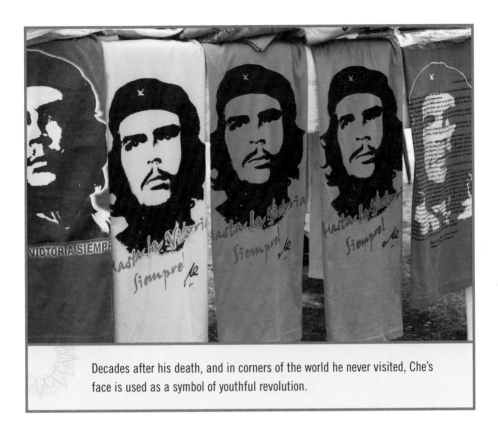

Decades after his death, and in corners of the world he never visited, Che's face is used as a symbol of youthful revolution.

He achieved nothing but disaster . . . Che presided over the Cuban Revolution's first firing squads. He founded Cuba's "labor camp" system—the system that was eventually employed to incarcerate gays, dissidents, and AIDS victims . . . He was killed in Bolivia in 1967, leading a guerrilla movement that had failed to enlist a single Bolivian peasant. And yet he succeeded in inspiring tens of thousands of middle class Latin-Americans to exit the universities and organize guerrilla insurgencies of their own. And these insurgencies likewise accomplished nothing, except to bring about the death of hundreds of thousands, and to set back the cause of Latin-American democracy—a tragedy on the hugest scale.[14]

But to anyone who knew Ernesto Guevara as a young boy, it would have seemed highly unlikely that he would have

become one of the twentieth century's best-known revolutionaries or terrorists, hated and loved by millions around the
world. But then again, Che was a person of many parts both
good and bad; too complicated to be shoehorned into just one
category.

A child of impoverished gentry, he was so wracked with
asthma that he studied at home until he was eight years old,
and yet he grew up to play soccer and rugby and to become
a tough soldier as well. Trained as a doctor to save lives, his
actions led to the death of many, including thousands that
he ordered to be executed. A poet and romantic, he was also
the author of one of the century's major revolutionary texts,
Guerrilla Warfare, a handbook used by rebels eager to learn
how to fight against government forces as well as the government they opposed.

He was a man of many hats. Argentine Marxist revolutionary. Politician. Author. Physician. Military theorist. Guerrilla
warrior. An examination of his life includes riveting stories of
Guevara traveling through Latin America, witnessing the overthrow of the Guatemalan government by the United States,
and helping Fidel Castro lead a revolution in Cuba, the rami-
fications of which are still being felt today. Che also traveled
to the Congo and Bolivia to lead revolutions against their dic-
tatorial regimes. These accounts provide the details of the real
story of Che Guevara—the story of the man on the T-shirt.

2

A Good Family

He was born Ernesto Guevara de la Serna on June 14, 1928, in Rosario, Argentina, the first child of Ernesto Guevara Lynch and Celia de la Serna y Llosa. (Some sources claim that he was actually born on May 14, and that his birth certificate was falsified to protect the fact that his mother was already pregnant when she married his father.) Perhaps ironically, the boy who grew up to become Che Guevara had been born to parents who were both full-fledged members of Argentine aristocracy.

His father, Ernesto, was born of Irish and Spanish nobility, a descendant of one of Argentina's oldest families whose great-grandfather had been one of South America's wealthiest men. (By the time Ernesto was born, however, the family had lost most of its money, and his father spent much of his time away from home attempting to bring back the family fortune via one unsuccessful business venture after another.) His mother was a direct descendant of Spanish nobles—one ancestor had been the Spanish royal viceroy of colonial Peru; another had been a famous Argentine general.

Ernesto Guevara as an infant with his parents in Argentina. Both his father, Ernesto, and his mother, Celia, were Argentine aristocrats.

Though Celia's parents died while she was quite young, her inheritance would help support the Guevara family for many years. She received a traditional Catholic school education but was also heavily influenced by the radical politics of her oldest sister, who raised her. Celia grew up to be a determined feminist, socialist, and free thinker, and it was she who had the greatest influence on Ernesto as he grew up.

For a time, though, it seemed questionable whether Ernesto would even get the opportunity to grow up at all. Just 40 days after his birth, he developed a severe case of pneumonia that almost killed him. Then on May 2, 1930, while the family was in San Isidro as Che's father was becoming a partner in a soon-to-fail shipbuilding firm, young Ernesto had his first asthma attack.

For the next three years, through June 1933, Ernesto suffered attacks daily. His parents were in agony, unable to do anything to alleviate their son's condition. They constantly moved around with their family, searching for a place to live that could help ease Ernesto's discomfort. They found it in the summer resort town of Alta Gracia, near the city of Córdoba, at the foot of the Sierra Chica. There, the thin, dry air helped to ease Ernesto's asthma flare-ups. Not that the attacks stopped completely or even became less frequent, but they did get less severe.

Living in Alta Gracia, Ernesto's asthma became manageable, thanks to improved climate, better medical care, and his parents' continued devotion. It was during this period of Ernesto's life that he and his mother became particularly close. Since he was too weak and frail to go to school, she taught him at home, and it was through her that Ernesto developed his lifelong devotion to books and an unquenchable intellectual curiosity.

Although Ernesto's father was often away on business, he too did what he could to comfort his son while he was ill. Many a night, Guevara Lynch would sleep sitting up on his son's bed, Ernesto reclining on his chest just so the boy would be able to breathe while he slept.

ALTA GRACIA

The majority of Ernesto Guevara's childhood was spent in the white, middle-class town of Alta Gracia. There, his father attempted to improve the family's financial fortunes, while his mother devoted herself to the care of her children: Ernesto; his two sisters, Celia and Ana Maria; and a brother, Roberto. (One additional brother, Juan Martin, was born in 1943.) For the family it was a time of relative security and tranquility, despite the fact that Argentina, as well as the rest of the world, was suffering through the consequences of the Great Depression.

At the beginning of the twentieth century, Argentina's economy ranked among the world's strongest. In 1913, for example, its per capita income was the thirteenth largest in the world—even greater than that of France. But with the onset of the Depression, a collapse in prices caused the nation's export revenues (largely beef and wheat) to plummet by almost 50 percent between 1929 and 1932. This caused a rapid growth in agricultural unemployment, which, accompanied by a growth in domestic manufacturing, drove millions of Argentines from the nation's rural areas to the cities in search of work. These new city residents, dark-skinned and thus looked down upon by the lighter-skinned upper classes, would form the ranks of a political movement that would shake Argentine politics and society for years to come.

That movement was still in the future. For five-year-old Ernesto, now relatively healthy for the first time in his life, his new surroundings were a wonderful place to explore. He made friends with the local children, the *barras*, playing as best he could between asthmatic attacks the normal childhood games of cops and robbers and war, and riding his bicycle through the hilly streets of Alta Gracia.

His mother was still convinced that her oldest and most beloved child was too ill to attend school, so his education took place at home, as she recalled in a 1967 interview.

I taught my son his first letters, but Ernesto was unable to go to school because of his asthma. He only attended the second and third grades on a regular basis; the fifth and sixth grades, he attended as much as possible. His siblings copied the school-work and he studied at home.[1]

If Ernesto's mother provided his early formal educa-tion, his father taught him an almost equally valuable lesson. From his dad, Ernesto learned the value of athletics, sports and competition, as well as the "conviction that through willpower alone he could overcome the limitations and hardships imposed by his illness."[2] Although any amount of physical exertion was difficult, Ernesto learned that it was the best possible remedy for his affliction. He played soccer, ping-pong and golf, learned to ride horseback and swim, and hiked in the nearby hills—anything to strengthen his lungs and body.

It proved to be a major aspect in his personality and devel-opment. His fierce determination to overcome his illness by sheer willpower led to his belief that through willpower he could overcome almost anything. Another factor in his per-sonality that developed during these years at Alta Gracia was his ability to communicate and associate with people on all levels of society.

Unlike many others of their social status, the Guevara children had friends at all levels: the children of the men who worked for his father's construction company; the poor chil-dren of the city's recent immigrants, who lived in shantytowns near the Guevara family home; middle-class children; and the upper-class children of the same elite status as Che's mother. Ernesto was comfortable with them all.

His carefree days of homeschooling and sports were soon to end. When he was nearly nine years old, education authori-ties from the Alta Gracia schools paid his parents a visit and ordered them to send him to school. In March 1937, Ernesto entered the second-grade class at the Escuela San Martin. He was nearly a year older than most of his classmates.

But if he was older than his peers, he was also more well-read. Because of his mother's influence, and due also to the long hours he had been forced to spend in bed because of his asthma, Ernesto had developed an intense and lifelong love of books and literature. He had already read the accepted children's classics of the time, including books like *The Three Musketeers* and *The Count of Monte Cristo* by Alexandre Dumas and *Treasure Island* and *Kidnapped* by Robert Louis Stevenson, as well as more adult-oriented books by Jack London, Jules Verne, Miguel de Cervantes, Anatole France, and Pablo Neruda. And thanks to his mother, he was also speaking French!

Despite his strong albeit nontraditional educational background, Ernesto's grades in school were good but not great. His third-grade teacher remembered him as "a mischievous, bright boy, undistinguished in class, but who exhibited leadership qualities on the playground."[3] One of the more memorable aspects of Ernesto's time in school during this period was his inclination to be the class show-off.

Whether this was to compensate for his sickliness is hard to say, but he quickly developed a fiercely competitive personality, always ready to engage in any activity that would earn him the attention of both teachers and classmates. He would drink ink out of a bottle, eat chalk, hang by his hands from a railroad trestle spanning a deep chasm, explore a dangerous mine, and even play "bullfighter" with an angry ram.

He quickly became a favorite of his classmates, becoming their leader both in and out of class, as his teacher Elba Rossi Oviedo Zelaya later remembered.

> I remember that the children followed him around a lot in the schoolyard; he would climb up a big tree that was there, and all the kids stood around him as if he were the leader, and when he ran the others would follow behind him; it was clear that

he was the boss. Perhaps it was the family, because it was a different sort of family; the kid knew how to speak better and all that. You could tell there was a difference. They never lacked anything, they were in another category; well, not that one could tell their category because they were snobbish, not at all.[4]

The Guevara family was anything but snobbish. Meals at their home were a free-for-all, as any visitor who arrived

JUAN AND EVA PERÓN

Juan Domingo Perón (October 8, 1895–July 1, 1974) was an Argentine general and politician who rode a wave of political turmoil to become elected three times as president of Argentina, the first time in 1946. Perón was overthrown in a military coup in 1955. After years living in exile, he returned to power in 1973 and served for nine months, until his death in 1974, after which he was he succeeded by his third wife, Isabel Martinez.

Perón and his second wife, Eva, were intensely loved by many of the Argentine people, especially the *descamisados*, the "shirtless ones," the low-income and working-class Argentines who made up Perón's political base. To this day, Juan and Eva (known affectionately as "Evita") are considered icons by the Perónist Party. Their followers praised their efforts to eliminate poverty and to dignify labor; their detractors, of which there are and were many, considered them little more than demagogues (political leaders who seek power by appealing to popular passions and prejudices) and dictators.

The Peróns gave their name to the political movement known as Perónismo, which in present-day Argentina is represented by the Justicialist Party. Of course, today, Eva Perón is the better remembered of the two, the subject of countless books and movies, as well as the award-winning stage musical *Evita*, which later became a hit movie with Madonna playing the role of Evita Perón.

at teatime or dinnertime was invited to stay and eat. Indeed, the family was known in the community as being somewhat "bohemian" or even odd. Celia helped to contribute to the family image; she was known as the first woman in Alta Gracia to drive a car on her own, to wear trousers, and even to smoke openly in public.

THE BEGINNING OF POLITICS

Even at this early age, the outline of Ernesto Guevara's personality was taking shape: intellectual curiosity, fierce willpower, and an interest in people of all different social strata. His last years in Alta Gracia would add one more part to the equation: a growing interest in politics.

From 1936 through 1939, the nation of Spain was wracked with civil war. A group of Spanish army generals led by General Francisco Franco, and backed militarily by the fascist governments of Adolf Hitler and Benito Mussolini, declared war on the democratically elected government of President Manuel Azaña. The war ended with the victory of the rebel forces, the overthrow of the Republican government, and the founding of a dictatorship by General Franco. (Though definitions vary, Fascists believe in single-party rule, and fascist regimes forbid and suppress criticism and opposition to the government.)

Ernesto Guevara, like many other young people of his generation, followed the war closely, hoping that the government of President Azaña would survive. In 1937, he hung a map of Spain on the wall of his room, using it to track the movements of both the Republican and Fascist forces.

He had personal reasons for his interest as well as a general hope that the "good guys" would win. His uncle, the poet Cayetano Cordova Iturburu, was in Spain working as a correspondent. In addition, as the war progressed and the position of the Republicans deteriorated, refugees from the war began to appear in nearby Córdoba and then in Alta Gracia itself. One family in particular, that of physician Jose Gonzalez

Aguilar, his wife, and three sons, struck up a friendship with the Guevara family that lasted for decades.

Ernesto would hear firsthand stories from the Gonzalez Aguilar family, as well as from other refugees, that further

Guevara poses at home in Argentina around 1934. It was around this time that the young boy had his first attack of asthma, a condition he suffered from his entire life.

deepened his commitment to the Republican cause. As Jorge G. Castañeda says in his biography of Guevara, "The Spanish Civil War—perhaps the last civil conflict until the Cuban Revolution to be broadly, almost unanimously, perceived as a battle between good and evil—was the decisive political event in Che's childhood and adolescence. Nothing else in those years would mark him as profoundly as the Loyalist struggle and defeat."[5]

His parents also supported the Republican cause. Dismayed at their defeat in 1939, they vowed to do what they could to stop any further spread of fascism. Ernesto's father founded a local branch of Acción Argentina, an anti-fascist organization that collected money for the Allies that were already at war with Nazi Germany, fought against any German penetration into Argentina, and kept watch against any signs of spying or espionage. Whenever Ernesto's father attended a meeting of Acción Argentina, 11-year-old Ernesto was sure to be there as well.

Their growing concern about fascism was a real one. Not only had Spain fallen to fascists, but Germany and Italy were controlled by fascists as well. The leadership in those countries was bent on ruling the world. Argentina, likewise, was seeing an emergence of a "nationalistic, Catholic, and virtually fascist right."[6] Indeed, under the rule of Ramón Castillo, Argentina, while officially refusing to take sides in World War II, silently supported Germany and the Axis powers, hoping that a German victory would provide new markets for Argentine exports as well as a supplier of arms for its own military.

A CHANGE

But while World War II continued overseas and Argentine politics grew increasingly complicated, everyday life continued for Ernesto and his family. In March of 1942, nearly 14 years old, Ernesto began high school, or *bachillerato*. Since Alta Gracia's schools only went as far as primary school, Ernesto was forced to travel by bus each day to Córdoba, 23 miles

(32 km) away, to attend the Colegio Nacional Deán Funes. Months later, during the summer of 1943 (Argentina's winter), the entire family moved to Córdoba.

It was the beginning of the end of the family unit. Ernesto's parents had been having problems with their marriage for some time; and although a period of reconciliation resulted in the birth of their final child, Juan Martin, in 1943, the estrangement between the two gradually deepened. The problem? Guevara Lynch's womanizing—it was an open secret that a good amount of the time he was away on "business" he was actually with a series of young ladies, whom he showered with presents paid for with money that his family badly needed.

Fortunately for the family, though, their time in Córdoba corresponded with a brief upswing in their financial fortunes. Guevara Lynch was doing so well in the construction business that the family was able to purchase a chalet in the hills overlooking the city. There, the family's eccentric lifestyle continued as before. Friends visiting Ernesto for the first time were astounded to come to a house where the furniture was usually buried underneath piles of books, where there were no regular mealtimes, and the children were allowed to ride their bicycles from the street directly into the house, through the living room, and out to the backyard.

Ernesto's time in Córdoba was filled with studies, sports, and friends. Despite his continuing problems with asthma, he began to participate heavily in team sports, especially rugby. He developed his interest due to his deep friendship with Tomás Granado, the youngest son of a railway conductor. Tomás Granado's older brother, Alberto, was the coach of the local rugby team, Estudiantes. Ernesto desperately wanted to play on his team, and despite his obvious physical handicap, Alberto took him under his wing for training. Soon enough, Ernesto had earned a place on the team.

As Guevera biographer Jorge G. Castañeda points out, rugby, a particularly rigorous form of football, provided Ernesto with two new challenges. It is known that strenuous exercise, such as one gets in a rugby match, is the single most common trigger for asthma attacks. For Ernesto, who already had the sunken, deformed chest common to serious asthma patients, overcoming the attacks and controlling them using a combination of an inhaler, epinephrine injections, and sheer force of will became a routine that he would carry with him throughout his life. In addition, the position that Ernesto played, half-scrum, involved less physical exertion than other positions and gave him an opportunity to develop new skills as a leader and strategist—skills that would come in handy in the years to come.

Alberto Granado and his fellow teammates were impressed with Ernesto's dedication and determination. They were so impressed, in fact, that they gave him the nickname "Fuser"—a contraction of *El Furibundo* and his mother's surname, de la Serna—for his aggressive style of play. Alberto was also impressed with Ernesto's intellectual curiosity. Waiting for practice to begin, Ernesto could be found leaning against one of the field's light posts, reading poetry by Pablo Neruda, John Keats, and Federico García Lorca, novels by Émile Zola, André Gide, and William Faulkner, and even the psychological studies of Sigmund Freud.

But despite his wide-ranging readings and his obvious intellectual abilities, his grades in school remained for the most part stubbornly mediocre. Perhaps this was due to his numerous extracurricular activities. They included sports, chess (which he had learned from his father), and a job with the provincial highway department. As his father said, "He was a wizard in his use of time."[7]

It seems likely that the deteriorating situation at home played its part as well. A family friend described the circumstances:

Family life was complicated. I remember when Juan Martin, the smallest of Ernesto's brothers, was born and I went to see him. I remember the house where they lived, [in] such disorder. . . . Celia was a very intelligent woman, very attractive as a person, one could speak with her very easily, but one did not feel that things were going well. . . . They even lived poorly: all right from a sociocultural point of view, but with very serious economic limitations.[8]

Perhaps in reaction, Ernesto began to dress and act in a way that made him stand out from the rest of his friends and classmates. His combination of "'devil-may-care' attitude, contempt for formality, and combative intellect"[9] were traits that he cultivated and retained throughout his life. Many felt that he enjoyed shocking people, as his friend and coach Alberto Granado confirmed:

He had several nicknames. They also called him "El Loco" [Crazy] Guevara. He liked to be a little bit of a terrible lad. . . He boasted about how seldom he bathed, for example. They also called him "Chancho" [The Pig]. He used to say, for instance: "It's been twenty-five days since I washed this rugby shirt."[10]

He was also displaying an increasing interest in politics, a sympathy and compassion for those less fortunate than himself, and a willingness to *fight*, although his reasons and goals remained uncertain, even to himself. In one famous anecdote, Granado had been arrested for attending a student anti-military demonstration. Ernesto visited him at the police station, and Granado suggested to him that he and his other friends organize further demonstrations.

Guevara's response? "Demonstrate in order to have the [expletive] beaten out of us? No way. I won't march if I'm not carrying a piece [a gun]."[11] As seen by biographer Jorge Castañeda, the incident demonstrates Ernesto's combativeness even at that age, as well as an understanding of how power works: Don't fight if you can't win. This would be an understanding that would serve him well throughout his life.

Unending intellectual curiosity, a willpower determined to overcome any obstacle, and a growing compassion for the poor and oppressed: Ernesto's personality was coming into sharper focus when, at the end of 1946, he finished high school. After spending that summer working for the roads department in Córdoba, he planned to study engineering in the city along with his friend Tomás Granado. But a chain of events was about to occur that would drastically change his plans and send his life in new and unexpected directions.

3

A Journey
of Discovery

In March 1947, while Ernesto stayed in Córdoba, the rest
of his family moved to Buenos Aires. Once again, the family's
finances were in bad shape, and on top of that, his parents
had finally decided it was time to split up. For the time being,
however, they moved into the apartment owned by Guevara
Lynch's elderly mother, Anna Isabel. That May, she fell ill, and
the Guevaras sent a telegram to Ernesto to let him know.

Two weeks later, another telegram was sent informing him
that his grandmother had suffered a stroke and was gravely
ill. Ernesto immediately quit his job and traveled to Buenos
Aires, arriving in time to attend her bedside for 17 days before
she died. Ernesto was beside himself with grief. His sister Celia
reported that "he was *very* sad; it must have been one of the
great sadnesses of his life."[1]

It seems likely that the loss of his beloved grandmother
drove Guevara to make a fateful decision. He would not return

to Córdoba to study engineering. Instead, he applied for and received admission to the Faculty of Medicine at the University of Buenos Aires. He would now study to become a doctor.

While his best grades in high school had been in the sciences, nothing in his past would have indicated an interest in medicine as a career. What had changed? His grandmother's death was obviously a factor. Others feel that his mother's bout with breast cancer was a reason. Perhaps it was a desire to find a cure for his own ongoing medical problems. Guevara himself was never entirely clear on his reasons, stating only that "I dreamed of becoming a famous investigator . . . of working indefatigably to find something that could be definitively placed at the disposition of humanity."[2]

He wholeheartedly plunged into his studies while holding down several part-time jobs. The most important of those jobs was at the Clinica Pisani, an allergy-treatment clinic. Oddly enough, he had first entered the clinic as a patient, but so impressed Dr. Pisani with his intelligence and curiosity that he offered him a position as an unpaid research assistant. Ernesto became so enthralled with the work being done there that he chose the study of allergies as his medical specialty.

By this time, his parents had settled into their home, one in its usual case of disarray. But it was different this time. Money was so tight that the older Guevara children were forced to find jobs to continue their education, and though their parents were legally married, they were physically separated. Ernesto Guevara Lynch's bed was now the living room sofa.

Ernesto was on the run so much that the chaos at home barely affected him. He was either working, studying at his Aunt Beatriz's apartment, or traveling—a newfound passion. At first he confined his trips to weekends hitchhiking back and forth between Buenos Aires and Córdoba. But he soon began going further and further away from home for longer and longer periods of time. It was becoming clear that while Ernesto enjoyed the study of medicine, it wasn't enough to keep him fully interested. He needed more.

He continued to play chess and continued to play sports. He also continued to feed his nearly insatiable appetite for books, expanding his interests beyond novels and poetry into

Although he opted to study medicine, Guevara had more pressing interests and passions. This photograph was taken around 1950, during Guevara's medical training.

LATINO INFLUENCE

Che Guevara, born in Rosario, Argentina, spent his life being influenced by, surrounded by, and married to fellow Latinos.

While growing up, many of his favorite writers were Latino poets: Pablo Neruda, Antonio Machado, Federico García Lorca, Gabriela Mistral, Cesar Vallejo, and Jose Hernandez. As he grew older, other Latino writers, not necessarily poets, became part of his reading life: Horacio Quiroga, Ciro Alegria, Jorge Icaza, Ruben Dario, and Miguel Asturias. For Guevara, who had literary dreams, it was the great Latino writers who showed him a way of writing and seeing the world that wasn't dependent on the great European masters.

It was with his friend Alberto Granado that he took the trip through South America that was immortalized in *The Motorcycle Diaries*. Both of the women who became his wives, Hilda Gadea Acosta, a Peruvian economist, and Cuban-born Aleida March, were Latinas. And of course, politically, his name will forever be tied to those of Raul and Fidel Castro, and to the success of the Cuban Revolution. From the beginning of his life to his last days fighting in the jungles of Bolivia, Che Guevara was continuously influenced and surrounded by Latino writers, politicians, military figures, and the "common" Latino people for whom he so courageously fought.

the worlds of history, philosophy and political science. He also began to write, composing poetry and keeping notebooks describing the books he had read and his thoughts and reactions to them.

He also managed to find time to maintain his friendships. On January 1, 1950, Ernesto set out on his first major road trip, using a bicycle equipped with a small engine. Along the way, he stopped in Córdoba to visit his old friend Alberto Granado, who had himself entered the field of medicine and was specializing in the study of leprosy, also known as Hansen's disease. After spending several days at the José J.

Puente leprosarium, where Alberto worked, Guevara continued his journey.

It was a life-altering ride. For the first time ever, Ernesto Guevara was outside of the middle-class cities in which he had grown up. He was now out in the country, where he could see at firsthand the effects of rural poverty. He was not only seeing but *experiencing* the way his country, as was the case in much of Latin America, was split in two. There were the cities, dominated by European immigrants. And then there was the countryside, where the nation's indigenous people, the Indians and the people of mixed European and Indian ancestry, known as the mestizos, lived in ways that hadn't changed in hundreds of years. It became clear to him that it was those people, the poor exploited peasants, whose hard labor was used to make the rich even richer.

FALLING IN LOVE

But along with an ever-expanding political consciousness came a change in Guevara's personal life. For the first time, the 22-year-old was in love. The target of his affection was the 16-year-old Maria del Carmen "Chichina" Ferreyra, the beautiful daughter of one of Córdoba's oldest and wealthiest families. It was not a romance destined to last.

The Ferreyra family initially found little to object to when the oldest son of the Guevara Lynch family began courting their daughter. Indeed, they were, at first, charmed and amused by his eccentricities, by his sloppy appearance and aggressive informality. But when Guevara began to pressure 16-year-old Chichina to marry him and travel with him throughout South America, the family had to draw the line. Their amusement turned quickly into opposition.

The couple continued to meet each other in secret, but it was no use. Chichina was a young girl, and unable to withstand her family's pressure to break off her relationship with Guevara. (Chichina's mother was so opposed to the match that she made a vow to Argentina's patron saint, the Virgin of Catamarca, that if her daughter stopped seeing Guevara, she would make a pilgrimage to the Virgin's distant shrine.) Guevara's dream of marriage seemed impossible.

Now 23, Guevara still had two more years of study before he could obtain his medical degree. He was, however, no longer sure that he wanted it. In love with a girl he couldn't have, bored with school, and filled with a desire to get back on the road, Guevara felt stuck and at loose ends, unsure what to do.

The answer came when he least expected it. For years, his friend Alberto Granado had dreamed of traveling the length of the South American continent. Now 30 years old, he knew that the time had come to make his dream a reality. But he didn't want to do it alone. There was only one person whom he knew was ready to drop everything and go. When asked, Guevara, fed up with school and everything else in his life, immediately accepted.

On January 4, 1952, the intrepid pair set off, riding a vintage 500 cc Norton motorcycle they nicknamed "*La Poderosa II*" (The Powerful II). Their first stop was the Argentine beachside resort of Miramar, where Chichina was vacationing with family and friends. As a last hopeful gesture, Guevara presented her with a gift, a puppy whose name translated to "Come Back" in English. She gave him $15 with which to buy her a scarf. With that exchange of romantic gestures behind him, Guevara and Granado continued their journey of discovery.

"I AM NOT THE SAME AS I WAS BEFORE"

It was an epic trek. When they left, they had very little money. Within a couple of weeks, they were nearly broke, relying on the kindness of strangers for their next meal or for a place to stay. But that was just what Guevara was looking for. He *wanted* a journey of adventure, where he would be forced to rely on his wits to survive—a trip that would force him into contact with the people of Latin America.

Bad news arrived just weeks into the journey when he received a letter from Chichina that had been forwarded to him at a jailhouse in Barlioche where he and Granado had been allowed to stay. In the letter, she informed Guevara that she had reached a final decision. She would not marry him and would not wait for him to return from his trip. In the diary Guevara kept of his journey, later published as *The Motorcycle Diaries*, he described his reaction.

> In the kitchen of the police station . . . I read and reread the incredible letter. Just like that, all my dreams of home . . . came crashing down. . . . I began to feel afraid for myself and started a tearful letter, but I couldn't write, it was hopeless to try. . . . I still believed I loved her until this moment, when I realized I felt nothing.[3]

Despite the pain he was suffering over the loss of his first love, Guevara was determined to continue his journey. Crossing the border from Argentina into Chile, Guevara and Granado took the opportunity to "reinvent" themselves, introducing themselves to some Chilean doctors they met on a ferry as "leprologists," doctors who specialize in the field of leprosy. They added to that by visiting a local newspaper, the *Correo de Valdivia*, presenting themselves as experts in leprosy with extensive research experience in neighboring countries. The paper believed them, and they walked away with a profile of themselves under the headline, "Two Dedicated Argentine Travelers on Motorcycle on Their Way Through Valdivia."

The pair struck once again in Temuco, where a February 19, 1952, *El Austral de Temuco* headline stated, "Two Argentine Experts in Leprology Travel South America on Motorcycle." Press clipping in hand, the two continued their journey through Chile, with Guevara generally driving and Alberto riding on the back.

While in the port city of Valparaíso, Guevara—who had said he had a doctor's degree in order to get food and shelter from the citizens—was asked to look in on an elderly servant woman suffering from severe asthma and heart problems. Guevara went to her room to do what he could, but knew when he saw her that she was dying and that there was little he could to help. He gave her what medicines he had to ease her suffering and left, deeply touched by what he had seen. He wrote in his diary:

> It is at times like this, when a doctor is conscious of his complete powerlessness, that he longs for a change: a change to prevent the injustice of a system in which only a month ago this poor woman was still earning her living as a waitress, wheezing and panting but facing life with dignity... There, in the final moments of people whose farthest horizon is always tomorrow, one sees the tragedy that enfolds the lives of the proletariat throughout the world... How long this order of things based on an absurd sense of caste will continue is not within my means to answer, but it is time that those who govern dedicate less time to propagandizing the compassion of their regimes and more money, much more money, sponsoring works of social utility.[4]

Unfortunately for Guevara and Granado, La Poderosa II was no longer in working order. To continue their trip, they had to find a new way to travel, as well as lodging and food to sustain them. Stowing away on the cargo ship *San Antonio*, they made it as far as the Chilean port city Antofagasta, where, forced to switch to another ship, they were discovered and left behind. Giving up on their idea of traveling by sea, Guevara and Granado began hitchhiking inland. Their first stop was the Chuquicamata copper mine, the world's largest open-pit mine, and the main source of Chile's wealth.

The mine, however, was not owned by Chile itself. It was owned and operated by U.S. mining companies such as Anaconda and Kennecott. So, while the mining companies themselves earned huge profits, Chile's share in the wealth was dependent on the monies it received from them, which fluctuated from year to year depending on the price of copper worldwide. To many Chileans, it was an unfair arrangement under which a few people grew rich while the workers themselves remained desperately poor.

The impact the mine visit had on Guevara equaled that of his visit to the dying woman in Valparaíso. While trying to catch a ride near the mine, he and Granado met a couple also trying to find a ride. The man was a miner who had just been released from prison, where he had been held for going on strike against the mine to protest working conditions. He told the two Argentine travelers that other strikers had disappeared shortly after their arrests and had probably been murdered.

The miner was a member of the Communist Party, which had been outlawed in Chile. Because of this, he had been unable to find work and was traveling with his wife (who had been forced to leave their children behind) deep into the mountains to a sulfur mine where working conditions were so horrific that his political beliefs wouldn't matter. Anyone willing to work there would be hired.

Once again, Guevara had come face-to-face with working-class life in Latin America. And once again, what he saw affected him deeply. He wrote in his journal:

> The couple, numb with cold, huddling against each other in the desert night, were a living representation of the proletariat in any part of the world. They had not one single miserable blanket to cover themselves with, so we gave them one of ours and Alberto and I wrapped the other around us as best we could. It was one of the coldest times in my life, but also one which made me feel a little more brotherly toward this strange, for me at least, human species.[5]

PERU

Guevara and Granado moved on to Peru, where yet another lesson awaited them. For the first time, they were in a country where a large indigenous population still existed, largely beaten down by centuries of poverty and white domination. The pair witnessed discrimination with their own eyes. Riding on crowded trucks, they found that while they were usually invited to ride in the front with the drivers, the more congested back of the truck was given over to the *cholos*, the Indians. As professionals, Guevara and Granado were considered to be the social superior of Peru's native population and were granted rights and privileges unimaginable to the cholos.

Because they were continuously out of money, they were forced to throw themselves at the mercy of Peru's Guardia Civil, the national police force, which had a station in every town. Their requests for help were almost never refused. On one occasion, the police chief responded to their need by shouting: "What? Two Argentine doctors are going to sleep uncomfortably for lack of money? It can't be,"[6] and insisted on paying for a hotel for them. It is unlikely that same police chief would have been as concerned about the needs of the indigenous people he was supposed to be serving.

Their travels continued. They visited Cuzco, one of the world's treasures—a colonial city built on top of the ruins of the ancient Incan Indian capital. There, their good luck persisted, as they found yet more people willing to help them along their way. Guevara ran into a doctor he had once met at a medical conference. The doctor gave them a jeep and driver who could take them for a visit to the Valley of the Incas, as well as free tickets for the train that would take them to the temple ruins of Machu Picchu.

The adventurers spent two days at Machu Picchu. There, they busied themselves exploring the stone remains of "the lost city of the Incas," playing soccer with the local citizens, and caging two free nights, stay at a local inn, which they left only when a group of paying American tourists arrived.

They returned to Cuzco by train, aghast at the conditions of the third-class wagon reserved for Indian passengers. Writing in his journal, Guevara expressed rage toward the American tourists visiting Machu Picchu. Busy traveling from tourist site to tourist site, they knew nothing about what was happening in the *real* Peru. Americans, he came to believe, not only exploited the resources of Latin America but cared nothing for the resulting poverty and oppression of the indigenous peoples.

This opinion amounted to the third "lesson" Guevara took away from his South American trip. Through the example of the dying woman, he'd come to believe that existing governments were failing in their responsibility to care for their people. From what he saw at the Chuquicamata mine,

LEPROSY

While traveling through South America and beyond, Ernesto Guevara enjoyed passing himself off as a renowned leprologist and took to visiting leprosariums.

Taken from the Greek *lepi* (meaning scales on a fish), leprosy, or Hansen's disease, is a chronic disease caused by bacteria, primarily of the skin and nerves in the hands and feet. Left untreated, leprosy can be progressive, causing permanent damage to the skin, nerves, limbs, and eyes. Contrary to popular belief, leprosy does not actually cause body parts to fall off.

In 1995, the World Health Organization estimated that somewhere between 2 million and 3 million people worldwide were permanently disabled because of leprosy. However, due to breakthroughs in research and multidrug therapy, leprosy is easily treated today. It has been estimated that within the last 20 years, 15 million people worldwide have been cured of the disease.

Although the enforced quarantine or segregation of patients is unnecessary, leper colonies still exist—in India alone, there are 1,000. One of the most famous leper colonies in the world actually existed in Hawaii—in Kalaupapa, on the island of Moloka'i. Inhabited by only a few elderly former patients, the colony is a National Historic Landmark.

he'd come to believe that American businesses were exploiting the natural resources of Latin America and taking away money that rightfully belonged to the people themselves. Now, having witnessed the treatment of the indigenous people of Peru, he came to feel a kinship, a connection, with the indigenous "conquered races"[7] that his forefathers had helped to defeat.

He'd also come to believe that despite the horrors perpetrated on the indigenous peoples by the European settlers, there was still a connection between the two groups. They were joined by a shared history exemplified by the mestizos—the people of mixed European and Indian ancestry. This connection, Guevara felt, should unite all Latin Americans to stand up and fight against what he saw as their common enemy: exploitation by the U.S. government and American businesses.

LEPERS AND LESSONS

Leaving the ancient homeland of the Incas, the intrepid duo traveled to the town of Abancay, where, in exchange for free room and board at the town hospital, they gave "lectures" on leprosy and asthma. Then, using a letter of recommendation from Guevara's doctor friend from Cuzco, they traveled deep into the country to visit the remote Huambo leprosarium.

It was a rough journey. Guevara's asthma began acting up again, and he grew so weak he could barely stand up. At the village of Huancarama, they asked the lieutenant governor if he could help them get horses so they could continue their trip. Anxious to assist the "renowned doctors" the men had been passing themselves off as, the man obliged, providing them with two.

As the pair rode off along with their guide, they saw they were being followed by an Indian woman and boy. When their pursuers caught up with Guevara and Granado, the men learned that the horses belonged to them. The governor had simply taken them to give to the Argentine doctors. Needless to say, after apologizing, Guevara and Granado returned the

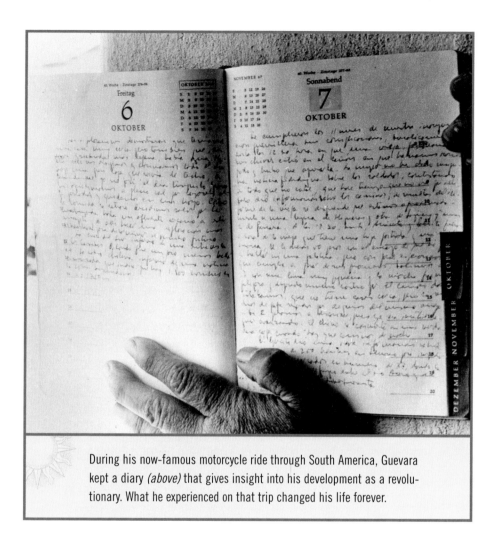

During his now-famous motorcycle ride through South America, Guevara kept a diary *(above)* that gives insight into his development as a revolutionary. What he experienced on that trip changed his life forever.

horses and continued the journey the best they could by foot. They stayed at the leper colony for several days, but with Guevara's asthma worsening, they were forced to move on to the town of Andahuaylas to find a hospital and medicine.

After recovering, their journey continued and included what was perhaps the roughest portion of their trip—a 10-day trek through the Andes towards the Peruvian capital of Lima on the Pacific coast. Broke and tired, as Guevara put it, "Our trip continued ... eating once in a while, whenever some charitable soul took pity on our indigence."[8] On May 1, after four long months on the road, they arrived in Lima, "penniless but content."[9]

Once again, their roles as renowned leprologists paid off. They introduced themselves to a *real* leprologist, Dr. Hugo Pesce, who arranged for them to stay in the Hospital de Guia for lepers. There, they were able to sleep in a real bed, eat, get their raggedy clothes washed, and rest up for the next leg of their journey.

They spent three weeks in Lima, time that allowed them to explore the city, catch up on letters from friends and family, attend hospital lectures, and, perhaps most importantly, be in one place long enough to receive money from their families.

Guevara also spent the time in long discussions with Dr. Pesce. Pesce, renowned in his profession, was also a prominent member of the Peruvian Communist Party. For Guevara, meeting Pesce was a revelation. Here, at last, was the first doctor he had ever met whom he felt was dedicating his life to the "common good."[10] And while Guevara was not yet a committed communist, the example Pesce set in putting beliefs into action gave him hope that he could do something similar with his own life.

Continuing on their way, Guevara and Granado decided they would travel to the San Pablo leper colony run by Dr. Pesce deep in Peru's Amazonia region. After a week's travel by bus, they transferred to the riverboat *Le Cenepa* for the seven-day journey to the region's capital city of Iquitos. On board, they spent their days talking with passengers and crew, playing cards, avoiding mosquitoes, and watching the passing landscape. Ill and exhausted, Guevara often asked himself the question that "would haunt him for the next fifteen years."[11] "The immense vault my eyes could see in the star-filled sky twinkled joyously, as if replaying affirmatively to the question rising from my lungs: is this worth it?"[12] For Guevara, the answer, despite everything, was a resounding "yes."

He spent two weeks at the leper colony, two weeks that allowed him to recover his health while realizing how lucky he was compared to those around him.

> One of the most interesting spectacles we have seen thus far: an accordian player who had no fingers on his right hand, replacing them with some sticks tied to his wrist; the singer was blind and almost all of them had monstrous faces due to the nervous form of the disease . . . A spectacle from a horror movie.[13]

GOING HOME

The great journey was coming to an end. Realizing that their goal of reaching North America was beyond their means, Guevara and Granado worked their way north through Colombia, reaching Caracas, Venezuela, on July 17. There, the friends would go their separate ways. Granado had decided to accept an offer from Dr. Pesce of a job at a leprosarium near Caracas; Guevara was given a seat on a plane transferring his uncle's racehorses from Buenos Aires to Miami. Guevara would board in Caracas when it stopped for refueling and fly with it to Miami, where, after unloading its cargo, he would fly home to Buenos Aires.

Engine problems forced Guevara to remain in Miami for nearly a month, where he scrounged for meals with his former girlfriend Chichina's cousin and earned extra money washing dishes. It wasn't until August 31, 1952, after eight months of traveling and a lifetime's worth of experiences, that Guevara returned home, determined to finish school quickly and get his medical degree. What he would do after that, of course, was anybody's guess.

4

A Revolutionary Is Born

The person who wrote these notes passed away the moment his feet touched Argentine soil again. The person who reorganizes and polishes them, me, is no longer, at least I am not the person I once was. All this wandering around "Our America with a capital A" has changed me more than I thought.[1]

Ernesto "Che" Guevara, *The Motorcycle Diaries*

Upon returning home, Ernesto Guevara immediately began contemplating when he would be able to leave again. His journey of discovery *had* changed him. There was more he wanted to see, more he wanted to learn about the world around him, and more he wanted to learn about himself. But first, he had to attend to some things in Buenos Aires.

He plunged into his studies, working as many as 14 hours a day preparing himself for the rigorous series of exams he would have to pass in order to qualify for graduation. The exams were given in series: He would be tested on 1 subject in October, 3 in November, and then 10 more in December. On April 11, 1953, he sat for his final exam. When he was finished, his first call was to his father, who picked up his phone and heard his son saying, "Dr. Ernesto Guevara de la Serna speaking."[2]

"My happiness was great," his father recalled. "But it lasted only a short time. Almost at the same time we found out he'd graduated as a doctor, he announced his new journey: this time his companion would be his old childhood friend Carlos 'Calica' Ferrer."[3] Apparently the call of the road was strong to Guevara, strong enough to pull him away from his home and family and new career. (His old boss Dr. Pisani begged him to stay, offering him a paid position, an apartment at the clinic, and a future as his assistant in allergy research. It wasn't enough for Guevara, who didn't want to "stagnate"[4] like Pisani.)

Guevara and Ferrer began planning their journey. They wanted to go through Bolivia, on to Venezuela, and then, maybe, Europe and India. All they needed was money. They began hitting up friends and relatives until finally, with $300 each, they boarded a train bound for Bolivia in July of 1953. Friends and family were there to wish them a safe journey. Guevara's mother said farewell with special sorrow, according to her daughter-in-law:

> When he left, I remember that his mother was sitting in an armchair; she took my hand and said to me, "Minucha, I am losing him forever, I will never see my son Ernesto again." Then we went to the train station, Celia was there, I remember that when the train pulled out Celia ran, ran, ran along the platform, next to the train.[5]

BOLIVIA

They arrived in La Paz, Bolivia, on July 11, 1953. Bolivia was one of the most Indian of nations in Latin America, as well as one of the poorest. For centuries, the majority Indian population had lived in deep poverty while a handful of white families made enormous fortunes from their control over the nation's tin mines and agricultural land.

But things were changing. In 1952, the Movimiento Nacionalista Revolucionario (MNR) had seized power, disbanding the army and nationalizing the mines. (To "nationalize" is to have the government take ownership of a privately held asset, such as tin mines, and make it a publicly held asset of the government—in effect, the property of all the people.) Next up on the government's agenda was agrarian reform law, which meant seizing the huge swaths of unused land owned by the wealthy landowners and turning it over to the peasants for their own use.

Not surprisingly, Guevara was fascinated by what was happening in Bolivia, writing to a friend that "Bolivia is a country which has given a really important example to America."[6] He spoke to the people, both in government and on the streets, learning as much as he could about what had happened and what people's hopes for the future were.

He visited the Bolsa Negra wolframite mine, which sat at an altitude of over 17,000 feet (5,182 meters). There, the mine's engineers showed Guevara and Ferrer the place where, during a strike just prior to the revolution, the mining company's guards had set up a machine gun and fired indiscriminately against the miners and their families. Now, the engineer pointed out proudly, the miners had won and the mine belonged to the state. Guevara could not help but be impressed.

But Guevara's good feelings about the Bolivian revolution quickly turned to disenchantment. Under pressure from the United States, still Bolivia's largest purchaser of tin, the new government decided to move slowly with land reform—much more slowly than Guevara thought was necessary.

In another incident, while waiting to meet with the minister of farmworker (*campesino*) affairs, Guevara and Ferrer witnessed a shocking scene that involved Indian farmworkers also gathered in the waiting room. Before these campesinos were allowed to meet with the minister, a ministry employee sprayed them with insecticide. Naturally, Guevara and Ferrer were horrified at the humiliation the campesinos, the "army"

Bolivian revolutionaries run through the streets of La Paz, Bolivia, on April 17, 1952. The revolution taught Guevara that practicing medicine was not the best way he could help people.

of the revolution, were forced to suffer. That evening, Che wrote in his journal:

> I wonder what the future of this revolution will be. The people in power fumigate the Indians with DDT to rid them temporarily of the fleas they carry, but do not resolve the essential problem of the insects' proliferation.[7]

It is apparent that as Guevara traveled further into Latin America, his identification with the indigenous peoples he saw grew deeper, as did his anger at the oppression and hardships they suffered. By observing the effects of hunger, poverty, and disease on the poor—seeing a poor parent accept that the death of a child unable to see a doctor was "just the way things were," for example—Guevara became more and more convinced that practicing medicine was not the best way to help. To do so, he would have to consider entering the field of armed struggle.

In mid-August, the travelers left Bolivia and moved on through Peru, visiting some of the places Guevara had seen with Alberto Granado. They ended up in the port city of Guayaquil, where, broke and in ill health, they languished for three weeks in the tropical heat before finally getting free passage on a ship bound for Panama.

There was now a change in itinerary. Instead of going on to Venezuela and meeting up with Alberto Granado, the two decided to go to Guatemala instead. It was somewhere Guevara had never been, a place of great beauty, and home to a large population of Indians. It would also prove to be the place that would send Guevara on the road leading to marriage and revolution.

GUATEMALA

He arrived in Guatemala on New Year's Eve, 1953, and would remain for more than eight months. Guatemala had a population of roughly 3 million inhabitants, the vast majority of which were poor Indians for whom life was a constant struggle for survival. With an economy based on agriculture—largely coffee, bananas, and cotton—it was one of the poorest nations in the region, dominated politically and economically by the

THE FILM *THE MOTORCYCLE DIARIES*

The film *The Motorcycle Diaries* tells the story of Guevara's 1952 journey, initially by motorcycle, across South America with his friend Alberto Granado. The screenplay is based primarily on Guevara's book *The Motorcycle Diaries*, with additional material taken from *Back on the Road: A Journey Through Latin America* by Alberto Granado.

The Mexican actor Gael Garcia Bernal threw himself whole-heartedly into the role of Guevara. He read every biography of the subject that he could find, traveled to Cuba to speak with Guevara's family, met with the revolutionary's travel partner Alberto Granado, and even spent weeks reading the works of José Martí, Karl Marx, and Guevara's favorite poet, Pablo Neruda—anything he could do to help him to understand the role.

Shooting took place on location in South America. Even the scenes in the San Pablo leper colony were shot in the same leper colony that Guevara had visited nearly 50 years earlier. The movie earned nearly universal critical and popular acclaim when it was released in 2004. Paula Nechak, writing for the *Seattle Post-Intelligencer*, summed up the view of many reviewers when she wrote that director Walter Salles "presents the evolutionary course of a young man who coincidentally became the dorm-room poster boy for an idealistic generation, and captures the lovely, heart-and-eye-opening ode to youthful possibility with affection and compassion."[*] It is a lovely film, one well worth seeing.

[*] Paula Nechak. "Motorcycle Diaries: On the Road with a Young Che." *Seattle Post-Intelligencer*, October 1, 2004. http://www.seattlepi.com/movies/193192_motorcycle01q.html.

United Fruit Company, which controlled the majority of the nation's land and politicians. But with the inauguration on March 15, 1951, of a new president, Jacobo Arbenz Guzmán, hopes ran high that change was about to occur.

Arbenz began a series of immediate social and economic reforms, vowing to bring change to a country where just 2 percent of the population controlled 70 percent of the land. He initiated an ambitious public works program that included new ports, highways, and hydroelectric plants. Then, on June 27, 1952, Arbenz signed into a law a land reform that allowed the state to appropriate uncultivated and unused lands from the large landed estates (*latifundia*) with compensation for the owners based on the land's declared value. Also included in the reforms was an income tax, laws guaranteeing the right of workers to a minimum wage and to collective bargaining, and the right to strike. Needless to say, neither the United Fruit Company nor the U.S. government was particularly pleased with Arbenz's reforms.

Guevara's guide to the Guatemalan political scene was Hilda Gadea Acosta, a Peruvian economist who had strong political connections as a member of the left-leaning political party Alianza Popular Revolucionaria Americana (American Popular Revolutionary Alliance, APRA.) It was through her that he met members of the Arbenz government, as well as activists working outside of it.

Guevara and Acosta's relationship, though, was more than just political. Actually, the two had met when friends fixed them up on a blind date. At that time, Guevara was in a bad fix: broke, suffering from a prolonged series of asthmatic attacks, cold, and hungry. Acosta immediately stepped in to help, finding him a place to live, getting him the medicine (and books) he needed and effectively getting his life back in order. Three and a half years older than Guevara, Acosta had strong Indian features he found very appealing, and they quickly became more than just friends.

For Guevara, it was a time of great excitement—both for political hopes and possibilities, and for the prospect of growing his relationship with Hilda. (It was also the time that he became known as "Che," due in large part to his frequent use of the Argentine diminutive interjection *che*, a slang casual

This photo of Jacobo Arbenz Guzmán *(left)*, standing next to Francisco Xavier Arana and Jorge Toriello, was taken in April 1945, nine years before Arbenz was forced to resign by the U.S. Central Intelligence Agency (CIA), a situation that deeply disturbed Che Guevara.

speech filler similar to "eh" or "like.") Nevertheless, the possibility that Guevara would use his medical degree in any professional capacity was fading with each passing day, done in by a combination of his inability to obtain a medical internship and his growing devotion to politics and his search for a way to remedy what he saw as the illnesses plaguing Latin America. He decided to use his time in Guatemala to "perfect himself and accomplish whatever may be necessary in order to become a true revolutionary."[8]

His time in Guatemala would soon be drawing to a close, however, as tensions within the country began to build. The United States had begun a policy of hostility and harassment against the Arbenz government, determined to force it out of power. But why would the United States want to overthrow a democratically elected government?

There were two main reasons. The first was economic—the United States was attempting to protect the financial interests of the United Fruit Company, which had come to see Guatemala as its own private banana plantation. The second reason was based on political ideology. The Communist Guatemalan Labor Party (PGT) was an influential part of the Arbenz government. To the United States, in the midst of a "cold war" with the Soviet Union, *any* participation by communists in *any* government, especially one so close to the borders of the United States, was a threat that needed to be stopped.

To the poor people of Guatemala, the ideological battle being fought between the United States and the communistic Soviet Union was irrelevant to their lives. For them, the PGT was one of the very few political parties that promised to improve their lives. They did not view themselves as political pawns to be used by either the United States or the Soviet Union in their geopolitical game of chess, but this did not matter to the larger power.

Pressure continued to mount when the Organization of American States, under the watchful eye of U.S. secretary of state John Foster Dulles, condemned the Arbenz government's actions on behalf of its people. Soon, the combination of pressure from the outside, dissension within the military, and Arbenz's own weaknesses proved to be too much. In June 1954, military forces commanded by Colonel Carlos Castillo Armas, directed and funded by the American Central Intelligence Agency (CIA), entered Guatemala from Honduras. On June 27, 1954, Jacobo Arbenz Guzmán was forced to resign from office.

Che was crushed by Arbenz's defeat and furious at the United States for what he saw as its opposition to any attempt at social and economic reform in Latin America. Convinced that the revolution could have been saved if "the people" had been given arms, Che was determined that in the future, the tragedy of Guatemala would not be repeated.

It was, he thought, impossible to negotiate with Washington while attempting the kind of reforms necessary in Latin America. Washington would not ever allow those changes of economic policy to take place without a fight. One would have to be prepared to fight for economic and social reforms, even at the cost of sacrificing one's own life. "It was Guatemala which finally convinced him of the necessity for armed struggle and for taking the initiative against imperialism. By the time he left, he was sure of this,"[9] wrote author Andrew Sinclair.

Days after the president's resignation, the new government began a crackdown of left-wing opposition figures. Hilda Gadea Acosta was among those briefly detained by the Bolivian police. Convinced that he was also in danger of being arrested, Guevara went to the Argentine Embassy and asked for asylum. After several weeks, he felt secure enough to leave the protection of the embassy walls to visit Acosta, who was still being held by Guatemalan authorities. The two made plans to meet after her release, and Che, with the protection of a safe-conduct pass, made his way to Mexico.

His early days there were not easy. He had no money, no work, and no friends. The only person he knew was a friend of his father, who bought him a camera. He began making a living taking pictures of U.S. tourists on the streets of Mexico City. By November, Acosta had joined him in Mexico, and through her, he began making contacts with other militants and politicians. Their relationship became closer, but Guevara still maintained a certain distance. She was not, as biographer Jorge G. Castañeda put it, "part of his plans."[10]

Che remained at loose ends in Mexico for months. But, as is so often the case, fate stepped in. In June 1955, Nico Lopez, an old acquaintance who had recently turned up in Mexico, introduced Ernesto Guevara to Raul Castro, a Cuban student and fellow exile who had recently been released from a Havana jail. Days later, Raul's brother arrived in Mexico, and Raul took his new friend to meet him. And so, as Jorge Castañeda so eloquently put it, "in the summer of 1955, Ernesto Guevara met Fidel Castro and discovered the path that would lead him to glory and death."[11]

5

The Revolution Begins

It seems likely Fidel Castro is a figure that Americans have been aware of most of their lives. A bearded man typically dressed in camouflage garb and given to long speeches, he is the object of hatred for a large number of Cuban Americans and conservative American politicians alike. Yet, when he first burst onto the scene in the early 1950s, he was seen by many as a freedom fighter and hero. What changed? To understand the next phase of Che's career, it is necessary to take a brief look at the life of Fidel Castro as well as the history of Cuba.

For the first half of the twentieth century, Cuba was a nation that was not entirely independent. Freed from Spanish colonialism by the United States during the Spanish-American War of 1898, Cuba briefly became a U.S. territory. Four years later, the country was given a choice: Remain a quasi-colony of the United States, or agree to the provisions of the Platt Amendment, which granted the United States the right to intervene in Cuba's internal affairs *whenever* the United States decided that public order was threatened.

Thus, for the next 50 years, in the words of Jorge Castañeda, "the island had experienced a sort of national purgatory. It had emerged from the hell of colonial rule without reaching the paradise of independence."[1] From the time of the Platt Amendment until 1933, the island's political life was marked by fraudulent elections, corruption, and constant meddling by the United States to keep order, protect its economic interests, and mediate between the various factions of the Cuban elite.

Finally, in 1933, an uprising by the *criollo* ruling classes and lower-ranking army officers led to a change that placed a reform government in place. It would not last though—the new government barely had time to tear up the hated Platt Amendment before it was overthrown by the military, led by Fulgencio Batista. A new constitutional government was put into place; a new labor force with strong sympathies to the Communist Party flexed its political muscle, and corruption and crime continued. The rich in the cities grew richer, while the poor in the countryside languished in poverty, as one president after another tried to bring order to a country whose wealth was based on large sugar plantations owned by a privileged few.

Finally, in 1952, another coup took place, once again placing Batista in charge. But this time the coup had little popular support, and opposition to the Batista regime grew. Some members of the military, as well as politicians and university students, joined a growing clamor for political and social change. Among those voices was a young Cuban lawyer named Fidel Castro.

Castro grew up well aware of the power the United States held over his country. The Oriente province where he grew up basically belonged to the United Fruit Company, which owned huge tracts of land as well as most of the area's sugar mills. There, Castro could witness that the Americans and their privileged Cuban employees led a life of luxury far beyond the reach of the average Cuban farmer. Indeed, Fidel's own father was completely dependent on the United Fruit Company—he leased the land that he farmed from it and was forced to sell his sugarcane back to their mills, at whatever price "the company" set.

Determined to change the way that Cuba was being ruled, Castro began speaking out against the government. In 1952, he ran for Congress, but when that election was cancelled in the aftermath of the coup that placed Batista in control of the government, Castro became convinced that the only way to bring about change in Cuba was with force.

He began to organize others in opposition to the regime. On July 26, 1953, he led an attack against the Moncada Barracks, a military barracks in Santiago de Cuba, hoping to spark a widespread revolt against the illegitimate Batista government. The revolt failed: 61 rebels were killed, and one-third of them were captured. Half of the men were tortured to death. A handful of rebels, including Castro, escaped into the countryside but were apprehended shortly thereafter.

While in prison, Castro wrote a speech that was later published and titled "History Will Absolve Me," which became the platform of the 26th of July Movement, the name given to the revolutionary organization created after the failed revolt. Castro was initially sentenced to death. But at the urging of Roman Catholic priests, Batista had abolished the death penalty just before Castro's scheduled execution.

Sentenced to 15 years in prison, Castro and the other rebels were instead released in 1955 after Batista bowed to pressure from Cuban political leaders, newspaper editors, and intellectuals. Once freed, Castro set out for Mexico City, where he could plan his next step.

It is important to note that at this stage in his career, Fidel Castro, perhaps the world's best-known communist leader, had not yet become a communist. It was Che Guevara who would eventually help push him down that political path.

Fidel Castro *(left)* and Che Guevara *(right)* are photographed in a Mexican jail in the summer of 1956, shortly after they met. Their alliance would bring Che glory and death.

When Castro and Guevara met in Mexico City in 1955, it was a life-changing meeting for both of them They talked late into the night, and by the time the sun rose the next morning, Guevara knew what he wanted to do, as he recalled in an interview years later.

> I met him during one of those cold Mexican nights, and remember that our first discussion was about world politics. After a few hours—by dawn—I had already embarked on the future expedition. Actually, after the experience I had had

walking through all of Latin America and the finishing touch in Guatemala, it wasn't hard to talk me into joining any revolution against a tyrant, but Fidel impressed me as an extraordinary man. He faced and resolved the most impossible things . . . I shared in his optimism. There was a lot to do, to fight for, to plan. We had to stop crying and start fighting.[2]

Fidel Castro provided Che with what he seemed to have been in search of: an opportunity to put his revolutionary ideals into practice. And although Che wasn't Cuban and had no personal stake in opposing the Batista government, he saw it as just one more example of a repressive regime installed and supported by the U.S. government and businesses. This led him to believe that Batista was a "U.S. puppet whose string needed cutting."[3]

The two men were an ideal match, each of them bringing something to the movement that the other lacked. One of Fidel's girlfriends, also a friend of Che, analyzed the pair:

Fidel's passion for Cuba and Guevara's revolutionary ideas ignited each other like wildfire, in an intense flair of light. One was impulsive, the other thoughtful; one emotional and optimistic, the other cold and skeptical . . . Without Ernesto Guevara, Fidel Castro might never have become a Communist. Without Fidel Castro, Ernesto Guevara might never have been more than an idealistic intellectual.[4]

TRAINING

Before fully committing himself to Castro's revolution, Che had to resolve his personal life. In July of 1955 he learned that Hilda Gadea was pregnant with his child. Although not wildly "in love" with her, Che was nonetheless determined to do what he believed was the right thing. On August 18, 1955, the couple married. In November, the couple went on a belated honeymoon, exploring the Mayan ruins at Palenque, Uxmal, and

SEEING LATIN AMERICA

Growing up in Argentina, and spending by far the majority of his life in Latin American countries, Guevara did not view being Hispanic in the same way as someone of Hispanic descent growing up in the United States does. He was not a Latino surrounded by non-Latinos. He was Hispanic to the core, with no doubts, no fuss, no muss.

But he did feel a pride in being Hispanic. And, from his travels through Latin America on a motorcycle in 1952, he came to a new understanding of Latin American history. He saw Latin America not as a collection of separate nations (Peru, Guatemala, Mexico, etc.), but as a single unit, united by a common language and culture. It was this understanding that led him to believe that all of Latin America needed to be liberated. The goal of a borderless, wholly united Hispanic America, united by its common Latino heritage, was what drove all of his later revolutionary activities. It was this dream of bringing about one Hispanic America that convinced him that he needed to leave the study of medicine and consider entering the world of politics and armed struggle in order to help his people become one.

Chichen-Itza. With that taken care of, Che devoted himself to preparing to join Castro's troops.

Castro had decided that the time had come for a military push into Cuba. His plan was to launch an invasion along Cuba's southeastern coast, and then have his troops move into the Sierra Maestra range, from where Castro would be able to launch a guerrilla war against the Batista regime. But to do that, he'd have to get his troops into shape—those already in Mexico, as well as those who were arriving almost every day from Cuba.

Training began slowly within Mexico City. It got more serious when Che and the rest of Castro's troops moved to a camp outside of Mexico City in Santa Rosa, and then later to a ranch at Chalco where a rigorous daily physical regime designed to get the men into shape along with military training nearly caused Che to drop out due to his asthma.

But he refused to let his condition get in his way, instead persevering and even attempting, on weekends, to scale Mexico's highest peak, Mount Popocatépetl. Although he never managed to make it to the top, his determination impressed everyone who saw him, including Fidel Castro. By the end of the training period, he was called "the best guerrilla of them all" and had been named as "chief of personnel"[5] by the troops' instructor, Colonel Alberto Bayo. Bayo recalled that:

> Guevara was ranked first in the class. He had the highest grade, ten, in everything. When Fidel saw the grades he asked me, why is Guevara always number one? Doubtless because he's the best. That's what I think, I said. I have the same opinion of him, Castro replied.[6]

There were two major interruptions to this period of training. On February 15, 1956, Guevara's daughter Hilda Beatriz was born. Then, on June 14, Fidel Castro and two companions were arrested in Mexico City by Mexican police agents. Within days, nearly all of the movement's members had been arrested, and on June 24, Guevara and 12 of his comrades were arrested at the Chalco ranch, charged with conspiring to assassinate Batista.

The charges didn't hold. Castro was released on July 24, and after much behind-the-scenes activity and not a few bribes, Che was released in mid-August, after 57 days of prison. It was the only time in his life that he would spend in jail prior to the evening before his execution.

With training completed, it was time for the invasion to take place. Guevara, secure in the knowledge that he had passed every physical test thrown at him, was ready to take the next step in his political and military career. This would, however, mean leaving his wife and daughter. Though Che's relationship with his wife had cooled to the point of indifference, his love for his daughter was deep and abiding. Nonetheless, the call to revolution outweighed any personal considerations. He would go with Castro to Cuba as the group's combat medic. Little did he know that role would change within moments of his landing on the Cuban coast.

SPANISH-AMERICAN WAR

The Spanish-American War was an armed military conflict between Spain and the United States that took place between April and August 1898. The stated public reason for the war was the liberation of Cuba from Spanish control. However, the United States had other motivations as well, which included a strong desire to build an empire of its own by annexing Spain's remaining overseas territories, such as the Philippines, Puerto Rico, and Guam.

A revolution in Havana prompted the United States to send in the warship USS *Maine* to make clear to Spain that the United States had a vested interest in Cuban affairs. When the *Maine* exploded in Havana harbor under mysterious circumstances, American interest in Cuba changed to outrage and a decision to declare war on Spain.

After easy American victories in the Philippine Islands and Cuba, the war was over. On December 10, 1898, the signing of the Treaty of Paris gave the United States control of Cuba, the Philippines, Puerto Rico, and Guam. Despite the fact that the war was nominally a war of "liberation," Cuba remained a virtual colony of the United States until 1959. The Philippines was granted independence in 1946, although the United States maintains military bases there. Guam and Puerto Rico remain unincorporated territories of the United States.

REVOLUTION

Before leaving Mexico, Guevara left behind a letter to be sent to his mother informing her of his plans and saying "goodbye" in the event that he was killed. In it, he said:

> And now comes the tough part, old lady; that from which I have never run away and which I have always liked. The skies have not turned black, the constellations have not come out of their orbits nor have there been floods or overly insolent hurricanes; the signs are good. They signal victory. But if they are mistaken, and in the end even the gods make mistakes, then I can say like a poet whom you don't know: "I will only take to my grave/the nightmare of an unfinished song."[7]

On November 25, 1956, the leaky cabin cruiser *Gamma*, loaded with 82 men, guns, and equipment, left Mexico for Cuba. The boat was scheduled to land on November 30 in conjunction with an uprising by the 26th of July Movement, which was already in place in Cuba.

Instead, the boat arrived three days later on December 2. Landing in difficult terrain, the invasion turned to disaster when, just three days later, it was attacked by Batista's troops. Many of the invading force were killed as Castro's men, frightened by their first experience of real combat, fled in confusion, abandoning their equipment and running for their lives.

In the ensuing panic, Che, who had received a superficial neck wound, found himself facing a momentous decision—was he a medic or a soldier? Guevara later wrote that it was during this first experience with combat that he laid down his medical supplies to pick up a box of ammunition dropped by a terrified companion. It was at that moment, it can be said, that Guevara made the final transition from doctor to combatant.

Only a small group of revolutionaries survived to make the trek deep into the Sierra Maestra to their planned rendezvous location. There, they regrouped, helped in no small part by the force of Fidel Castro's confidence and willpower, as well as the assistance of local peasants sympathetic to the rebels' cause. In less than three weeks, the group was ready for their first military action, a successful attack on a military position in La Plata. It was just the morale booster that the bedraggled troops needed.

Che and his companions would spend the next year and a half in the Sierra Maestra and eastern Cuba. With the group withdrawn to the mountains, many people outside Cuba wondered whether or not Castro was alive. While in the Sierra Maestra, supplies and morale were often low, and Che, living in a remote, muggy region of the country, suffered asthma attacks, malaria, and an allergic reaction to mosquito bites that left his body covered in painful cysts. These were, as he remembered later, "the most painful days of the war."[8]

But as the war continued, the once physically frail doctor became a vital part of the rebel army, a man who "convinced Castro with competence, diplomacy and patience."[9] Not just a soldier, he set up factories to manufacture grenades, built ovens to bake bread for his men, taught new recruits military tactics and political philosophy, and reached out to the surrounding communities to teach illiterate campesinos, the peasants on whose behalf he was fighting, to read and write.

There was, however, another side to Che Guevara that emerged in the Sierra Maestra. The man *Time* magazine dubbed "Castro's Brain," the man who was promoted by Fidel Castro on July 21, 1957, to the rank of Comandante (the only other Comandante was Castro himself), the trained doctor and fighter for the poor—was also a man of great ruthlessness, who would do anything he felt necessary to keep his troops together and defeat the forces of Fulgencio Batista.

Che was a tough leader, demanding the same level of dedication and discipline from others that he demanded of himself. He was also capable of taking that toughness to the extreme and was unforgiving of anyone who decided to leave his command. Deserters were treated as traitors, and Che was

Che Guevara rides in the Sierra Maestra as part of Castro's rebellion against the Batista government in Cuba. It was during this time that he gained Castro's utmost respect.

known to send out execution squads to hunt down those who desired to go AWOL, that is, "absent without official leave." To Guevara, anyone who deserted was a risk to the revolution —someone who could be forced to reveal information about the rebels' positions and organization to Batista's forces.

Guevara was also personally capable of summarily executing anyone he felt was a traitor to the cause. The case of Eutimio Guerra is a good example. Guerra, a peasant who had served as a guide for Castro's rebels, had been captured by the Cuban army and released on the condition that he serve as an informant of Castro's whereabouts. The information that he provided had led to the deaths of numerous rebels, and when his treachery was discovered, there was in Che's mind only one solution to the problem.

For many years, historians wondered exactly who had pulled the trigger on the first traitor to be executed by the Cuban rebels. Guevara's private diary revealed the truth.

> The situation was uncomfortable for the people and for [Eutimio Guerra] so I ended the problem giving him a shot with a .32 [-caliber] pistol in the right side of the brain, with exit orifice in the right temporal [lobe]. He gasped a little while and was dead. Upon proceeding to remove his belongs I couldn't get off the watch tied by a chain to his belt, and then he told me in a steady voice farther away than fear: "Yank it off, boy, what does it matter. . ." I did so and his possessions were now mine. We slept badly, wet and I with something of asthma.[10]

This passage is a remarkable look into the mind of Che Guevara. Note the complete detachment with which he is able to describe the execution, the coolly scientific medical description of the bullet wounds he himself had caused. Not a moment's self-doubt about killing another human being. The doctor trained to heal was now a soldier willing to kill for his cause.

Yet at the same time, Guevara saw his role as a teacher as well as commander. During breaks between military engagements (and in the kind of guerrilla war Che and Castro were fighting there were a lot of breaks), Guevara would entertain his men by reading to them from his favorite books—works from Robert Louis Stevenson, Miguel de Cervantes, and the great Spanish lyric poets. His combination of toughness and support for his men led Castro to describe his right-hand man as intelligent, daring, and an exemplary leader who "had great moral authority over his troops."[11]

Guevara relished his time with his troops, a time when he was able to give of himself completely and become not just an individual, but a part of a whole. Everybody was there for everybody else, everyone suffered equally, and when one man needed help one day, the next day it was his turn to help somebody else. This sense of a shared cause was something that Che had been searching for his entire life, and he found it deep in the mountains of eastern Cuba.

There were times when Guevara himself was in deep need of assistance from his men. In February 1957, Che began suffering a series of asthma attacks. On February 25, "a day of water and bombs"[12] as he referred to it, Che and his troops awoke to the sound of nearby mortar blasts and machine-gun and rifle fire. Certain that the Cuban army was searching the area, the rebels were forced to break camp after dark. With just chocolate and condensed milk to eat, the men marched in the rain for two days, with Che seriously weakened by asthma attacks as well as constant vomiting from bad pork he'd eaten days earlier.

Castro ordered the troops to go up into the mountains for safety, but Che was too weak to proceed. "I couldn't keep up with the pace of the march, and I was constantly lagging behind."[13] Assisted by his men and carried half the way, Che arrived with his fellow soldiers at a place of sanctuary called Purgatorio. Without medicine, Che was unable to continue. Castro ordered the rest of the troops to proceed while sending

Cuban guerrillas raise their rifles during the revolution. Che quickly became an exemplary soldier, as well as a commander.

a peasant guide to the nearest town to buy medicine. Che was to remain at Purgatorio, in the company of an escort.

For two days, Che hid out at Purgatorio, barely able to breathe and on constant alert for the sounds of the Cuban army. Finally the medicine arrived, but it was only one dose. With no other option available, by sheer force of will, Che managed to make it to the appointed rendezvous with the rest of his troops, arriving five days late. Days later, with the arrival of badly needed medicine, he recovered and was able to continue.

At the same time Che was struggling for survival at Purgatorio, the Batista regime that he was fighting so hard to replace suffered a staggering blow when the *New York Times* published Herbert Matthew's 1957 interview with Fidel Castro. Ever since Castro and his men had invaded Cuba and disappeared into the Sierra Maestra, the Batista regime had been telling the world that Castro was dead, and the rebels defeated and in disarray. But now the *New York Times* was telling a completely different story.

> Fidel Castro, the rebel leader of Cuba's youth, is alive and fighting hard and successfully in the rugged, almost impenetrable vastness of the Sierra Maestra, at the southern tip of the island... [T]housands of men and women are heart and soul with Fidel Castro and the new deal for which they think he stands... Hundreds of highly respected citizens are helping Señor Castro ... [and] a fierce Government counterterrorism [policy] has aroused the people even more against General Batista... From the look of things, General Batista cannot possibly hope to suppress the Castro revolt.[14]

It was the beginning of the end of the Batista regime. The media in other countries picked up on the interview, and Castro and his army of rebels became heroes around the world; they were seen as freedom fighters standing up against a corrupt and repressive government, living and fighting with "the people" they hoped to lead. Victory was soon to come, and with it a new set of challenges. What happens to rebels when they become the leaders?

6

Victory and Its Aftermath

The Battle of Uvero on May 28, 1957, which earned Che his role as Commandante, proved the rebel army's growing military prowess. That battle, which pitted 80 rebels against 53 Cuban soldiers, cost the Cuban army 14 dead, 19 wounded, and an additional 14 taken prisoner. The rebels, meanwhile, suffered only 6 casualties.

It was Che himself who led his men into battle. As one of his closest aides, Harry "Pombo" Villegas, recalled, "He was a man who liked to take the lead in combat, to set an example; he would never say, go and fight, but rather, follow me into combat."[1] Then, after the battle was over, Che the doctor would replace Che the fighter as he tended to his men's wounds.

The battle itself, while relatively minor in the grand scheme of things, did accomplish two things. It gave the rebels firm control of an area that the Cuban army could not enter.

And it proved once and for all Che's bravery and tenacity in battle, leading Castro to name him Commandante.

From that day forward, Che took on a wider and wider range of responsibilities, not only in military training and strategy, but in policy disputes within the leadership of the 26th of July Movement itself. As Jorge Castañeda said of Che's new role, "He was no longer a foreign physician who could be expelled at any time, but a *commandante* who had won his star in combat and who now participated fully in the Revolution's substantive debates."[2]

And as the policies of the revolution moved away from liberal reform toward a more radical agenda, it was Che, the Marxist theoretician, who provided the intellectual basis for the change. It was Che who urged Castro not to compromise his ideals by aligning himself with other rebel organizations in order to achieve victory.

It was, as Castañeda noted, during this period of the struggle that Che became known as "the guerrillas' 'Communist' or radical."[3] He also made his name as a superb organizer of men, a leader able to gain the support of the peasants within the territories he won in battle by building badly needed schools, clinics, ovens, and hospitals that the Cuban government had for years neglected to provide.

Che also began to reach out to the outside world from the Sierra Maestra. He launched a newspaper, *El Cubano Libre*, and was instrumental in creating the pirate radio station Radio Rebelde in February 1958. The radio station proved vital to the success of the revolution by broadcasting news to the people with statements from the 26th of July Movement and providing radio and telephone communication between the growing number of rebel columns moving across the island. Ironically, Che got the idea for the station while he was in Guatemala and personally witnessed the effectiveness of CIA-supplied radios in bringing down the government of Jacobo Arbenz Guzmán.

THE BATTLE TURNS

The turning point for the rebels was the Battle of Las Mercedes (July 29–August 8, 1958). This was the last battle of Operation Verano, the summer offensive launched by the Batista government in a desperate attempt to destroy the rebels once and for all. The battle itself was a trap, designed by Cuban general Cantillo to lure Castro's guerrillas into a place where they could be surrounded and destroyed.

But Che, sensing the trap, used his column to halt the movement of Cantillo's forces. (Years later, Major Larry Bockman of the U.S. Marine Corps would describe Che's tactical achievement in this battle as "brilliant."[4])

Instead of surrendering, Castro offered a cease-fire, which Cantillo accepted. During the cease-fire, Castro's forces used the opportunity to escape back into the hills.

The battle, although technically a victory for the Cubans, turned out to be a staggering defeat. By talking with Castro instead of killing him and his men, the Cuban army was revealed to be weak and uncertain of its mission. Batista lost confidence in his senior generals, the junior officers lost confidence in their commanders, and demoralization swept through the Cuban army.

Castro, on the other hand, viewed the results of the battle (despite having suffered the loss of one-quarter of his army) as proof that the Cuban army had lost the will to fight. The time was now right to leave the mountains and bring the war directly to the cities of Cuba. Castro himself would lead one force against Guisa, Maso, and other towns on the east side of the island. Che would lead the second force, directed at the provincial capital of Santa Clara, the fourth-largest city in Cuba and the last major obstacle standing between the rebels and the capital city of Havana.

For six weeks, there were times when Che's men were completely surrounded, outgunned, overrun, and seemingly on the verge of defeat. But under his inspired leadership they persevered, in what some have called one of the more remarkable accomplishments in modern warfare. Soon, victory piled on top of victory, and as 1958 came to a close, Che's men began to make the final push into Las Villas Province and Santa Clara.

Che directs orders to one of his soldiers during the Battle of Santa Clara. The battle proved to be the decisive victory for Castro's army.

Three columns were sent against Las Villas Province. One column, lead by Jaime Vegas, was caught in an ambush and completely destroyed. Camilo Cienfuegos's column directly attacked a local army garrison at Yaguajay. Che's column took up positions around Santa Clara. Guevara was determined to take the city himself without any assistance from Cienfuegos, as heard in a broadcast over Radio Rebelde:

> The enemy is concentrated in the usual places . . . I heard you tell Fidel that you were going to take Santa Clara and I don't know what the hell else, but don't you butt in there because that's mine.[5]

On December 28, 1958, Guevara's column traveled along the road from the coastal port of Caibarien to Camajuani, which lay between Caibarien and Santa Clara. The rebels had easily captured Caibarien, and that, combined with the crowds of peasants cheering them on along their way, contributed to the feeling that victory was within reach. Government troops guarding the army garrison at Camajuani deserted their posts without incident, and Guevara's column marched into Santa Clara, arriving at the city's university on its outskirts at dusk.

Che had an unsentimental detachment to battle that allowed him to work single-mindedly toward his goals. He could inspire his men to acts of untold bravery, a quality that ultimately proved to be decisive. He illustrates the dynamic in this passage from his memoirs:

> I rebuked a soldier for falling asleep in full battle, and he replied that he had been disarmed for having fired without orders. I answered with my customary dryness: "Go win yourself another rifle, go up to the front line unarmed . . . if you are capable. In Santa Clara [I was] encouraging the wounded . . . a dying man touched my hand and said, "Do you remember, *commandante*? You sent me to get a weapon . . . and I won it for myself." It was the soldier who had fired without orders,

who would die minutes later, and he seemed happy to have proven his bravery. That's what our Rebel Army is like.[6]

The battle to take the city lasted three days. Initial reports broadcast by the government stated that Guevara had died in the fighting and that Batista's forces had won a stunning victory. That proved not to be the case. Che, with a force of just 300 men, defeated the defending army forces commanded by Colonel Casillas Lumpuy and captured an armored train sent by Batista to reinforce the city with supplies of badly needed ammunition, weapons, and other equipment.

With the capture of the train, the battle was over. Army officers began asking for a truce, while ordinary soldiers began to join with the rebels, saying that they were tired of fighting against their own people. On New Year's Eve 1958, Radio Rebelde broadcast the first reports that Santa Clara had been taken by Guevara and his men. And with the weapons captured by Guevara, Castro's troops were now in the driver's seat, with more firepower at their command than that of any other group that had been fighting Batista.

The next day, January 1, 1959, Cuban president Fulgencio Batista, having learned that his generals were negotiating a separate peace with the rebel leader, fled to the Dominican Republic. One week later, on January 8, Fidel Castro and his second-in-command, Ernesto "Che" Guevara, triumphantly entered Havana and were greeted by ecstatic crowds. The military aspect of the revolution was over. The social and political revolution had just begun.

REMAKING CUBA

Although there had been numerous groups fighting in opposition to the Batista regime, it was Castro and his 26th of July Movement that declared victory and assumed the reins of government. And according to their later retelling of the days of revolution, they were solely responsible for the overthrow of Batista; it was their achievement alone. Che, the intellectual engine of the revolution (continuing this analogy, Castro was the political engine), later described how the lessons of the Cuban revolution were now applicable throughout all of Latin America:

> We have demonstrated that a small group of men who are determined, supported by the people and without fear of dying ... can overcome a regular army...There is another [lesson] for our brothers in America, economically in the same agrarian category as ourselves, which is that we must make agrarian revolutions, fight in the fields, in the mountains, and from here take the revolution to the cities, not try to make in the latter without a comprehensive social content.[7]

This lesson, learned by Che in the Sierra Maestra, was one he would take with him for the rest of his life. Ultimately, it bore tragic consequences for him as well as a whole generation of would-be revolutionaries.

Two days after Castro and Guevara entered Havana, Che's parents, sister, and brother, Juan Martin, arrived in Cuba. It was their first reunion in years, and while his family was proud of his accomplishments, they were still concerned about his future. Would he stay in Cuba? Would he return to medicine? Would he come home to Argentina?

The answer, of course, was that his job in Cuba was not complete. He would stay in Havana and work with Castro to complete their revolution. After that, who knew? He explained how he saw his future to his father, saying:

> As for my medical career, I can tell you that I deserted it a long time ago. Now I am a fighter who is working in the consolidation of a government. What will become of me? I don't even know in which land I will leave my bones.[8]

Two weeks later, his wife, Hilda Gadea, and their daughter, Hilda Beatriz, arrived in Havana. It was the first time he

Che stands amid guerrilla rebels during the Cuban Revolution.

had seen them in years, and he was forced to greet them with some unwelcome news. During his time in the mountains, he had become involved with another woman, Aleida March, with whom he had been living since late 1958. Che asked for a divorce, and on May 22, his marriage to Gadea ended. Days later, on June 2, 1959, he married Aleida March.

With his personal life taken care of (and for Che, his personal life was always a distraction from his real life of politics and social rebuilding), Guevara could settle in to concentrate on his work. His commitment to Cuba's future grew even more personal on February 2, 1959, when he, along with all other foreigners who had spent at least two years fighting Batista, was granted full Cuban citizenship. No longer the "foreigner," he was now working to rebuild and remake his own country. His first task was to sweep away the remnants of the Batista regime.

During the rebellion against Batista's dictatorship, the general command of the rebel army had introduced into the liberated territories the nineteenth century penal law commonly known as the *Ley de la Sierra*. This law included the death penalty for extremely serious crimes, whether perpetrated by the dictatorship or by supporters of the revolution.

In 1959, the revolutionary government extended the law's application to the entire nation and to those it considered war criminals—individuals captured and tried after the revolution. According to the Cuban Ministry of Justice, this extension of the law was supported by the majority of the population and followed the same procedures as those of the Nuremburg Trials held by the victorious Allies after World War II.

To implement this plan, Castro named Che commander of the La Cabana Fortress prison, for a five-month tenure (January 2 through June 12, 1959). It was Guevara's responsibility to purge the Cuban army of Batista supporters. His other task was to consolidate the victory of the rebels by exacting justice against those deemed to be traitors, *chivatos* (informants), or war criminals.

In his post as commander of La Cabana, it was Che who would review the appeals of those convicted during the revolutionary tribunal process, a process that lacked what unbiased observers would call due process. Nonetheless, Che felt that the government needed to do whatever it took to protect itself from those who might wish to keep it from reaching its goals—including executions by firing squads. In a

February 5, 1959, letter to a friend in Buenos Aires, Guevara defended this death penalty, saying that "the executions . . . are not only a necessity for the people of Cuba, but also an imposition by the people."[9] It has been estimated that between 200 and 700 people were executed under his watch.

He had other responsibilities as well. Che was a member of the Tarara Group, whose members included the more left-wing members of the new Cuban government. It was the Tarara Group that helped to create the machinery that would become the state security forces within Cuba. In addition, the group began to organize efforts to export the revolution to Panama, Nicaragua, the Dominican Republic, and Haiti. Che played a part in all four attempts, none of which were ultimately successful.

There were other assignments as well. The government began considering the problems of land reform within Cuba. For centuries, huge areas of unused land had been owned by a very small number of powerful landowners. For the Cuban economy to work—if the peasants were going to be able to lift themselves up from the poverty in which they had always lived—a system had to be found to shift the ownership of land from the few to the many. To do so, of course, would anger the nation's wealthiest citizens, as well as arouse the suspicions of the United States, which equated any kind of land reform as communistic and something to be stopped.

But for Che, land reform was the next logical step forward in the ongoing Cuban Revolution. He said that:

> Cuba's anti-popular regime and its army have now been destroyed, but the dictatorship's social system and its economic foundations have yet to be abolished. Many people from before are still working within the nation's structures. To protect the fruits of the revolutionary victory and allow for a continuous development of the revolution, we must take another step forward.[10]

And if all that wasn't enough, Che was assigned one more task—the training of a new army, one built on the ideology of the revolution itself. The new army became the cornerstone of the new regime, due in no small part to Guevara's success in instilling the new soldiers with the fervor and motivation necessary to support the revolution.

GOING ABROAD

It is not surprising that Guevara, one of the main public faces of the new government, came under his share of criticism—even from Castro himself. For months following the victory over Batista, Che had been inching closer and closer to the PSP, the Popular Socialist Party—the Communist Party of Cuba. But Fidel Castro, the leader of the revolution, was in the process of trying to convince the United States that while he was a reformist, he was not a communist and neither was his government. (It is not clear, and historians are uncertain, as to whether or not Castro was indeed a communist at that point and was trying to placate the United States until his power was more secure.)

Whichever may be the case, relations between Castro and Guevara became slightly strained during this time as various political factions within the revolutionary government jockeyed for position and power. Castro made a decision to remove Che from the scene, at least for the moment, and sent him on an overseas tour. This move allowed him to at least *appear* to be distancing himself from Che and his Marxist sympathies, easing the concerns of both the United States and some of the more conservative members of Castro's 26th of July Movement.

CHE'S WORLD TOUR

There were, of course, other reasons for Castro to send Che on tour—he was, in fact, probably the only close aide that Fidel could count on to make a good impression of the revolution on those abroad. Che left Cuba on June 12, 1959, and visited 14 countries over a three-month period.

In Egypt, he met with President Gamal Abdel Nasser, the hero of Arab nationalism. He went to India. He spent 12 days in Japan, where he participated in negotiations aimed at expanding Cuba's trade relations with that nation. When visiting the Asian nation, he also made a secret visit to the city of Hiroshima, where he was shocked to see the damage caused by the American military's use of the atomic bomb 14 years earlier during World War II. Everywhere he went, everything he saw, served to further convince him of the rightness of the Cuban Revolution and the need to expand it throughout the developing nations—what became known as the "Third World."

Indeed, by the end of his tour, Ernesto Guevara was now a man fully committed to the revolution—everything else came in second place. He described his political evolution in a letter to his mother, Celia:

> My old dream of visiting all countries is now coming true. . . A sense of the big picture as opposed to the personal has been developing in me. I am still the same solitary person who continues to seek his path without any help, but now I have a sense of my historical duty. I have no house, wife, children, parents, or brothers; my friends are friends as long as they think like me, politically, and yet I am happy, I feel important in life—not only a powerful inner strength, which I always felt, but also an ability to influence others and an absolutely fatalistic sense of my mission which frees me from all fear.[11]

RETURNING HOME

Upon his return to Havana on September 10, 1959, it was clear that Castro had amassed more political power for himself and was continuing his gradual move toward Marxism. The government had begun the land seizures included in the land reform law but was wavering on the compensation that would be offered to the affected landowners. Instead of direct cash payments, the government was now offering low interest "bonds"—a move that put the United States on alert.

It was at this point that the first relatively organized resistance against the revolutionary government came into shape. A group of wealthy cattlemen at Camaguey mounted a campaign against the land redistributions and enlisted as part of their cause the newly disaffected rebel leader Huber Matos, who, along with the anti-communist wing of the 26th of July Movement, joined them in denouncing the "Communist encroachment."[12]

At the same time, the Dominican dictator Rafael Trujillo (one of the right-wing leaders that the Tarara Group had unsuccessfully attempted to overthrow) was offering assistance to the "Anti-Communist Legion of the Caribbean," which was training in the Dominican Republic. This was a multinational force made up mostly of men from Francisco Franco's fascistic Spain and Cubans unhappy with the Castro government, as

THE EXPLOSION OF *LA COUBRE*

On March 4, 1960, the French freighter *La Coubre*, carrying munitions from the port of Antwerp, exploded twice while being unloaded in Havana harbor. At the sound of the first explosion, Guevara raced to the site and ran into the burning ship, providing medical assistance. Over 100 people were killed in the explosion, and hundreds of others were wounded.

The next day, a funeral cortege wound its way through the streets of Havana, with Fidel Castro and Che Guevara at its head. Later, while Castro was addressing the crowd from a balcony, a Cuban photographer named Alberto Korda found a good spot from which to take pictures. Looking through his viewfinder, he took a photograph of Che Guevara. It is this photograph of Che—his eyes seemingly staring boldly into the future, his face a portrait of outrage—that quickly became a photographic icon. It is this photo that stares out boldly from T-shirts, posters, and hundreds of other media, displaying Che Guevara as the ultimate revolutionary icon.

Che Guevara and his bride, Aleida, pose with wedding guests after the ceremony on June 2, 1959. Raul Castro stands at the far left with his wife, Vilma.

well as Croatians, Greeks, and other right-wing mercenaries, all plotting to topple the new Cuban government.

Trujillo's Anti-Communist Legion ultimately did invade Cuba. Castro, though, was waiting for them when they landed near the Cuban city of Trinidad, and they were easily defeated. Not all of the legion's fighters had been sent to Cuba, however. One of those left behind was an 18-year-old military cadet named Felix Rodriguez. The same Felix Rodriguez who, eight years later, would lead the CIA-backed search in Bolivia for one Ernesto "Che" Guevara.

These developments, combined with growing American antipathy toward the Cuban government, prompted Castro to expand the program to "clean house" of counter-revolutionaries within his government. Che was appointed as director of the Industrialization Department of the National Institute of Agrarian Reform (INRA) on October 7, 1959, and named as president of the National Bank of Cuba on November 26, 1959.

As Jorge Castañeda points out, with those appointments, two of the Cuban Revolution's most important governmental positions were placed in the hands of a radically pro-Soviet Argentine physician with little knowledge of economics. But by doing so, Castro was sending a definite message to both the United States as well as the old Cuban ruling class about who, exactly, was running the country.

For 14 months, Che was in charge of the central bank, responsible for Cuba's monetary policy, reserves of foreign currency, and long-range economic strategy. He was also involved in rebuilding the Cuban army and engaging in the nation's diplomatic affairs, as well as writing and giving speeches defending the revolution. His main focus, however, was the bank, where he was a tireless worker known for arriving at his office mid-morning and staying until 2:00 A.M. or 3:00 A.M. every night.

Perhaps his most notorious achievement in his role as president of the National Bank involved the issuance of Cuban currency. As in other nations, each piece of paper money contains the signature of the person in charge of currency, in this case Ernesto Guevara. Showing the same lack of respect for formalities that had distinguished him in his youth, the currency was not signed "Ernesto Guevara." It was simply signed "Che." He answered criticism of this by a Cuban correspondent by replying:

> If my way of signing is not typical of bank presidents . . . this does not signify, by any means, that I am minimizing the importance of the document—but that the revolutionary process is not yet over, and, besides, that we must change our scale of values.[13]

Che maintained his informality in other ways as well. Even as president of the National Bank of Cuba, he greeted visitors to his office dressed in his military olive green fatigues, his feet firmly on top of his desk.

Despite his outward appearance, Che was deadly serious about his work. His goal was to achieve a diversification of Cuba's economy, which for too long had been dependent on sugar and other agricultural products. On the other hand, while he recognized the importance of a strong economy, he viewed traditional capitalism as a "contest among wolves" where "one can only win at the cost of others." He desired to see the creation of a "new man and woman"[14] who would work together to create a worker's paradise.

As an important part of this process of fostering a sense of unity between the individual and the masses (with the individual working for the good of all), Guevara was a strong proponent of volunteer work for the masses. The first project began on November 23, 1959, with the construction of the Ciudad Escolar Camilo Cienfugeos in Caney de Las Mercedes. For several months, Che would fly to Las Mercedes every Sunday, where, along with workers from a nearby shoe manufacturing plant and soldiers from the rebel army, he helped to build the school named after his friend and fellow rebel, the late Camilo Cienfuegos.

He didn't stop there. He helped to bring in the sugar harvest in December. He worked in construction and in textiles. Not only did Che enjoy, as always, the opportunity to work alongside "everyday" Cubans, he believed that he was setting an example for all Cuban citizens to emulate. For the revolution to succeed, he believed that all Cubans had to do their part, to become involved in continuing the work of the revolution.

Volunteer weekends quickly became the fashion throughout Cuba. Unfortunately, the "volunteer" weekends ultimately became virtually mandatory weekends, used to extend people's working hours without pay. Those who didn't "volunteer" soon found themselves under scrutiny by the government and were suspected of being "counter-revolutionaries." Che did not live long enough to witness this corruption of his idealistic dream of workers happily coming together to build a new society.

There were times, of course, when Che allowed himself activities outside those of government. He wrote constantly, publishing books and articles promoting his revolutionary ideals. Encouraged by his wife, Aleida, he also began exploring the world of classical music. This was something new to him, and he quickly developed a strong passion for it—Beethoven was a particular favorite. And although he was a communist revolutionary, he did allow himself the occasional luxury, including a good Cuban cigar. Montecristo No. 4's were his smoke of choice.

After one year in power, the new Cuban government appeared to be making progress on all fronts. There would, however, soon be new challenges. Despite Castro's best efforts, Cuba's relationship with its neighbor to the north, the United States, was rapidly deteriorating. Would the Cuban government suffer the same fate as that of Guatemala just seven years earlier?

Breaking Away

Relations between the United States and the new Cuban government did not deteriorate overnight. It was a slow process, caused by a lack of understanding on both sides, Cuban reforms, U.S. fear of communism and Soviet influence, and sheer political necessity.

U.S. president Dwight D. Eisenhower officially recognized the new Cuban government immediately after the 1959 Cuban Revolution. But relations between the two governments began to cool almost immediately as the U.S. government became increasingly concerned both by Cuba's land reforms and its nationalization of U.S.-owned industries.

Fidel Castro visited the United States along with a delegation of representatives as part of a "charm offensive" to convince America of his government's good intentions.

Although President Eisenhower made sure he was out of town when Castro visited Washington, D.C., the Cuban leader

Fidel Castro is greeted in Washington, D.C., on his public relations visit to the United States. His meeting with vice president Richard Nixon did not go well, and the United States eventually ended trade relations with Cuba.

did meet with then vice president Richard Nixon to outline his plans for reform.

The meeting did not go well. Nixon later told Eisenhower of his certainty that Castro was either himself a communist or a communist dupe, "incredibly naïve"[1] about the influence of communists within his government. After this meeting, the United States began to impose gradual trade restrictions on the island. On September 4, 1959, U.S. ambassador Philip Bonsal met with Castro to express "serious concern at the treatment being given to American private interests in Cuba both agriculture and utilities."[2]

Che expected the United States to resent Cuba's determination to take control of the industries and resources it had "given away" to foreign companies. In a speech given months earlier entitled "Social Projections of the Rebel Army," he spelled out in detail what Cuba needed to do to reform its economy as well as what the U.S. response would be. He spoke of the need for Cuba to move beyond an economy based on sugar exports, of the need for rapid industrialization, and of the need for the country to liberate itself from American economic domination.

As Jon Lee Anderson described the speech:

> He warned that the United States was not going to take kindly to what he was proposing. "We must be prepared for the reaction of those who today dominate 75% of our commercial trade and our market. To confront this danger we must prepare ourselves with the application of countermeasures ..." To industrialize, Cuba must first rescue its natural resources, which had been given over to "foreign consortiums by the Batista dictatorship." The nation's mineral wealth and electricity should be in Cuban hands, and the state telephone company, an ITT subsidiary, should be nationalized ... "National recovery will have to destroy many privileges and because of that we must be ready to defend the nation from its declared and its disguised enemies."[3]

As the economic reforms continued, trade restrictions on Cuba increased. The United States stopped buying Cuban sugar and refused to supply Cuba with badly needed oil—two devastating blows against an already shaky Cuban economy. In February 1960, President Eisenhower gave authorization to the Central Intelligence Agency (CIA) to organize, train, and equip Cuban refugees as a guerrilla force to overthrow Castro. As it had done in Guatemala, the United States wanted to replace a leader it didn't want with a leader it *did* want, regardless of the wishes of the Cuban people themselves.

The two nations began a diplomatic game of tit for tat, each Cuban move requiring an American response and each American response requiring a new move by the Cubans. Each time the Cuban government nationalized American properties, the American government responded, resulting in the prohibition of all exports to Cuba on October 19, 1960. Cuba was now cut off economically from its formerly largest trading partner and from most U.S. allies as well, who bowed to American pressure to stop trade with Cuba.

Cuba was left with just two choices. It could either placate the United States by stopping the reforms it believed were necessary to rebuilding an independent Cuba. Or, it could continue the reforms and find an ally strong enough to support Cuba against American economic and military pressure. The Cuban government decided on the latter, gradually consolidating relations with the Soviet Union and reaching trade and military agreements with the United States's greatest adversary. In response, on January 3, 1961, the United States withdrew diplomatic recognition of the Cuban government and closed its embassy in Havana.

Historians still argue over what caused Castro and his government to turn away from the United States and the West and turn to the Soviet Union. Was it only because U.S. actions forced Cuba to do so in order to survive? Was Castro always a communist who hid his political beliefs until he felt the time was right to reveal them? Did American actions force Castro into making the move toward communism faster than he wanted to? These answers remain up for debate, but one thing is certain. Fifty years after the fact, U.S. economic sanctions against Cuba are still in place, and diplomatic relations still do not exist between the two nations.

On January 20, 1961, John F. Kennedy, just 44 years old, was inaugurated as president of the United States. CIA plans for an invasion of Cuba were already in place. Kennedy, though wary of the possibility of success, gave in to political pressure to prove his "toughness" against a communist adversary and gave the go-ahead for the invasion to proceed. It was the biggest mistake of his young presidency.

The anti-Cuban forces, made up of CIA-trained Cuban exiles, invaded Cuba at the Bay of Pigs on April 17, 1961. Just three days later, it was over—the Cuban military had captured or killed all of the invaders. For the United States, it was a huge embarrassment. For Cuba, it was a smashing success. The country had successfully stood up to the United States and won. The invasion served to strengthen Castro's rule, by uniting the Cuban people with him against the U.S. government.

Three months after the invasion, during an economic conference of the Organization of American States in Punta del Este, Uruguay, Che Guevara sent a "thank you" note to President Kennedy through Richard N. Goodwin, a young secretary at the White House. It read, "Thanks for the Playa Girón (Bay of Pigs). Before the invasion, the revolution was shaky. Now it's stronger than ever."[4]

Che himself had nothing to do with the fighting in the invasion, having been ordered by Castro to a secretly arranged command post in Cuba's western Pinar del Rio province, where he fended off a decoy force sent by the United States to distract from the primary invasion force. Ironically, Che was severely wounded during this deployment when a bullet grazed his cheek after his pistol fell out of his holster and accidentally went off. The danger to his life came not from the wound itself, but from the anti-tetanus injection given to him by his military medics, which led to a toxic shock reaction. Che later joked, "My friends almost managed to do what my enemies couldn't: I nearly died!"[5]

With the failure of the Bay of Pigs invasion, the United States began to formulate new plans aimed to destabilize the Cuban government. These activities were known as "The Cuban Project" (also as "Operation Mongoose"). It was a coordinated program of political, psychological, and military sabotage, involving intelligence operations as well as assassination attempts on key political figures. (A U.S. Senate Select Intelligence Committee report later confirmed at least eight attempted plots to kill Castro between 1960 and 1965, as well as additional plans against other Cuban leaders.)

Why was the United States so determined to bring down the Castro government? A big reason was that many Americans feared the Soviet expansion of communism or socialism anywhere in the world. Castro's early land reforms and nationalization itself appeared to be a threat to American interests. And then, when Cuba made the decision to ally itself openly with the USSR, the situation was regarded by the United States as completely unacceptable. (Soviet involvement with Cuba also defied the centuries-old Monroe Doctrine, a U.S. policy stating the nation's opposition to European powers getting involved in South American matters.)

This is not to say that Cuba was blameless in regards to its increasingly tense relationship with the United States. In September 1962, the Cuban government saw significant evidence that the United States was planning a second invasion, including a U.S. congressional resolution authorizing the use of military force in Cuba if American interests were threatened. Under pressure, Cuba felt the need to respond, but it was a response that brought the United States and Russia closer to war than in any other time of the Cold War.

The Soviets made a proposal to the Cuban government that would allow Russian nuclear missiles to be placed in Cuba. By doing so, the Soviets would gain a powerful military beachhead just 90 miles (145 km) from the United States. By allowing it to happen, Cuba hoped to forestall any potential U.S. invasion.

Che, who was practically the architect of the Soviet-Cuban relationship, played a key role in bringing the Soviet nuclear-armed ballistic missiles to Cuba. It was Guevara who went

Che Guevara meets with Soviet premier Nikita Khrushchev in the USSR in December 1961. After the U.S. government rebuffed Castro, he turned to the Soviet Union. Che signed an agreement with Khrushchev to allow Soviet missiles on Cuban soil.

to Russia on August 30, 1962, to negotiate and sign the final agreement, entitled "Agreement Between the Government of Cuba and the Government of the USSR on Military Cooperation for the Defense of the National Territory of Cuba in the Event of Aggression."

By September 6, with Che back in Havana, the United States was already detecting a Soviet military buildup in Cuba, but was as yet unaware of the extent of the threat. Che was thrilled with the new agreement, certain that with the protective umbrella of Russian nuclear missiles in Cuba, the United States would be powerless to stop the ongoing revolution. As one classified intelligence cable paraphrased him, "The United States cannot do anything but yield."[6]

On October 14, U.S. reconnaissance saw the missile bases being built in Cuba. The U.S. military was placed on the highest alert, and navy ships were sent to establish a blockade around Cuba to keep out any further military shipments from the Soviet Union. For the next two weeks, the world watched and waited as tensions between the two nuclear powers continued to mount.

It looked entirely possible that the all-out nuclear war that had been feared for so long would actually take place, as both sides refused to back down. Finally, on October 28, 1962, the Soviets blinked. An agreement was reached by which the nuclear missiles would be dismantled in Cuba in exchange for a no-invasion agreement from the United States. The Cuban Missile Crisis had come to an end.

The Cubans were furious at the Soviet Union for giving in to the United States and taking back their nuclear missiles, feeling that they had been betrayed by their closest ally. Che, the man who had put together the agreement that brought the weapons into Cuba in the first place, was particularly upset, telling a British Communist Party daily paper:

> If they [the United States] attack, we shall fight to the end. If the rockets had remained, we would have used them all and

directed them against the very heart of the United States, including New York, in our defense against aggression. But we haven't got them, so we shall fight with what we've got.[7]

It is chilling to realize that Guevara was prepared to let millions of American citizens be killed in a nuclear war in order to protect Cuba from invasion.

Indeed, it seems that Che Guevara was willing to go to any length to defend the Cuban government. It was Che who set up Cuba's first "labor camp." This camp, the first of many, was established in the hot, remote, rocky Guanahacabibes Peninsula, on the westernmost tip of Cuba. It was there that the "enemies" of the revolution were sent for rehabilitation, enemies that soon included dissidents, homosexuals, and, in later decades, AIDS victims. They were in effect prison camps, which Che attempted to justify in a speech to the Ministry of Industries:

> We send to Guanahacabibes those people who should not go to jail, people who have committed crimes against revolutionary morals, to a greater or lesser degree, along with simultaneous sanctions like being deprived of their posts, and in other cases not those sanctions, but rather to be reeducated through labor. It is hard labor, not brute labor, rather the working conditions are harsh but they are not brutal.[8]

POSITIVES

It is important to note that despite everything—the constant threat of invasion from the United States and its economic sanctions, as well as the repressiveness, paranoia, and brutality of the Cuban government itself—the revolution was in many ways a success for many Cubans.

Advances were made in education. Before 1959, for example, 40 percent of all children between the ages of 6 and 14 were not able to go to school. By 1961, that number had fallen to 20 percent. Che, always aware of the importance of

THE GREAT PROLETARIAN CULTURAL REVOLUTION

Just as Che Guevara's political sympathies were shifting from the Soviet Union and its Eastern Bloc allies to Asia and the People's Republic of China, China was on the verge of entering one of the most cataclysmic events of its modern history—the Cultural Revolution.

It was launched by Mao Zedong, the chairman of the Communist Party of China, on May 16, 1966. Mao, who had been laying low during a power struggle in the upper levels of the Chinese government, alleged that liberal "bourgeoisie" elements were dominating the party and insisted that they be removed through post-revolutionary class struggle. His means of removing the liberal elements from the party: millions of China's youth, who were formed into groups called the Red Guards.

Fanning out throughout the country, the Red Guards attacked everything they considered to be an enemy of the state and of the revolution. Schools were closed, and historical reserves, artifacts, and sites of interest were destroyed because they were thought to be the source of the old ways of thinking. Millions of people in China suffered attack as well. Those identified by the Red Guard as spies, "running dogs," or "revisionists" (such as landowners) were subject to attack, imprisonment, rape, torture, harassment, and abuse, while hundreds of thousands were murdered, executed, and starved or worked to death. Millions were forced to leave their homes and moved to the countryside to work in the fields. Standard education was abandoned in place of the propaganda teachings of the Communist Party of China.

The chaos of the Cultural Revolution lasted from 1966 through 1969. It has been estimated that in the rural areas of China alone, 38 million people were persecuted and between 750,000 and 1.5 million people killed, with just as many permanently injured. It would be interesting to know what Che would have thought of the catastrophe caused by the Great Proletarian Cultural Revolution, had he lived to see the results.

education and literacy, led an education campaign throughout Cuba that reduced illiteracy to just 3.9 percent. By 1965,
the percentage of Cuban children enrolled in school was 50
percent higher than any other Latin American country.

In addition, hospitals and clinics were built around the
country, bringing health care to all. Vaccine campaigns were
organized, and large numbers of physicians, both male and
female, were trained to replace those who had left after the
revolution. For many Cubans, the revolution had brought
about a better standard of living, a better life.

For the next two years, Che continued to work in Cuba to
better the lives of ordinary Cuban citizens while speaking out
around the world against what he saw as the oppression of the
masses by the few. In December 1964, he traveled to New York
City as head of the Cuban delegation to speak at the United
Nations, where he gave in impassioned address on behalf of
those whose lives he hoped to improve.

In his speech, he recited from the Second Declaration
of Havana, calling Latin America a "family of 200 million
brothers who suffer the same miseries."[9] Their story, Guevara
vowed, would be written by "the hungry Indian masses,
peasants without land, exploited workers, and progressive
masses."[10]

To Che, the conflict was a struggle of ideas, to be fought
by those who had been mistreated under capitalism and were
previously considered too weak and inconsequential to fight
back. Things had changed, Che asserted. "Yankee monopoly
capitalism,"[11] now saw those once-marginalized people as
their "gravediggers."[12]

It was now, Che declared, that the "anonymous mass"[13]
would begin to write its own history "with its own blood"[14]
and reclaim those "rights that were laughed at by one and
for all for 500 years."[15] He ended his remarks to the UN by
hypothesizing that this "wave of anger"[16] would "sweep the
lands of Latin America."[17] He suggested that the labor masses,
those who "turn the wheel of history," for the first time were

"awakening from the long brutalizing sleep to which they had been subjected."[18] This clarion call for the masses to rise and stand up against their economic and social oppressors would

Che Guevara holds a press conference. Che's world tour inspired him to commit to the revolution even more deeply.

reverberate throughout the world as he continued to speak and travel.

At the end of 1964, Che set out on a three-month tour that brought him to the People's Republic of China, the United Arab Republic (Egypt), Algeria, Ghana, Guinea, Mali, Dahomey, Congo-Brazzaville, and Tanzania. During this trip, Che wrote a letter to Carlos Quijano, editor of a Uruguayan weekly, which was later published and retitled *Socialism and Man in Cuba*.

The letter was a call for the creation of a new consciousness, status of mode of productivity, and role for the individual. Che ended the essay by declaring that "the true revolutionary is guided by a feeling of love," and calling on all revolutionaries to "strive every day so that this love of living humanity will be transformed into acts that serve as examples."[19]

It was in Algiers on February 25, 1965, that Che made what turned out to be his last public appearance on the international stage when he delivered a speech on African-Asian solidarity. In it, Che criticized the Soviet Union and its socialist bloc allies for not doing enough to help the developing nations of Latin America, Asia, and Africa, and for not supplying the arms necessary for the poor in those parts of the world to rise up against their oppressors.

Having directly and publicly criticized the Soviet Union, Cuba's primary financial backer, when Che returned to Cuba on March 14, 1965, he was met at the airport by a grim-faced Fidel and Raul Castro. Two weeks later, Che dropped out of public life and then vanished altogether. At first in Cuba, and then around the world, the question arose: Where was Che Guevara?

8

The Road to Martyrdom

His whereabouts were a mystery for nearly three months. The man who was considered second-in-command only to Fidel Castro himself, the very public face of the Cuban Revolution, disappeared from public life. What was going on?

Che's disappearance has been attributed to many factors. The primary one was that Castro himself was furious at Che for compromising Cuba's relationship with the Soviet Union by attacking it so publicly. Indeed, for some time, Guevara, who had been one of the driving forces in the development of the relationship between Cuba and the Soviet Union, had been reassessing his attitude toward that nation and its Eastern Bloc allies.

Che had grown disillusioned by the Soviet Union's refusal to support Cuban-style revolutions throughout Latin America, and by what he saw as social and economic compromises made by the Soviet Union that were leading it away from the pure Marxism in which he believed. On the other hand, the People's Republic of China, led by Mao Zedong, practiced the kind of communism in which he did fervently believe, along with a shared conviction that a "new man and woman" could indeed be created who would work together to create a better society not for financial reward, but because it was the right and moral thing to do.

The problem for Che, Castro, and Cuba was this: Despite the fact that both the Soviet Union and the People's Republic of China were communist countries, relations between the two were not good. For the Soviet Union, it was unacceptable that someone like Che, with a strong belief in the Maoist form of communism, could be a part of the Cuban government that received most of its financial and military backing from the Soviet Union.

Besides the politically untenable position in which Che found himself, there were other factors at play in his disappearance from the public eye. In many ways, his work in Cuba was finished. The idealism of the revolution was giving way to compromise in order to achieve financial growth. In December 1964, for example, the government announced that it would be beginning a pilot program that included such "capitalist" ideas as contractual salaries, profit sharing, and prizes for workers.

Castro, while giving a speech in Santa Clara against a giant photo of Che as a backdrop, made it clear that Che's idealism had no place in Cuba's next stages of development.

> Nor [can we have] idealist methods which conceive of all men obediently following the concept of duty, because in real life we cannot think like that. . . It would be absurd to try [to convince] the great mass of men who cut cane to make their best effort out of duty, regardless of whether they make more or less.[1]

Once again, during his period of invisibility, Che was reassessing his personal life. Despite having had four children with his second wife, Aleida, their marriage was in trouble, due largely to Guevara's continued insistence that the cause of justice and revolution come first in his life—everything else was secondary.

Put all those factors together, combine them with Che's continued wanderlust, and it's obvious that by the spring of 1965, it was time for him to leave Cuba and go to work helping others to revolt against oppressive governments. He would go to Africa, where he hoped to apply the lessons learned in the Sierra Maestra to an ongoing rebellion in the Congo, which Che saw as having tremendous revolutionary potential. It would prove to be a disaster.

THE CONGO

Guevara had been warned that the Congo was not the right battlefield for him. Egyptian president Gamal Abdel Nasser, with whom Che had close relations, saw his plans as "unwise" and warned that although he might see himself as a "Tarzan" figure, "a white man among blacks, leading and protecting them,"[2] he was doomed to failure. Regardless of the warnings, Guevara, along with his second-in-command Victor Dreke and 12 other Cubans, arrived in the Congo on April 24, 1965. Approximately 100 Afro-Cuban soldiers joined them soon afterward.

Che went to the Congo to help support the Marxist Simba movement, which had emerged from an ongoing crisis in the Congo. Guevara and his men worked for a time with guerrilla leader Laurent-Desire Kabila, who had led an unsuccessful revolt several months earlier. Disappointed with the discipline of Kabila's troops, Guevara would dismiss him, finding him impossible to work with.

The political situation in the Congo was tremendously complicated, but suffice it to say that Che found himself facing not only other rebel forces, but the Congo National Army backed by mercenaries from South Africa, Cuban exiles, and the CIA. They were able to monitor his communications, which allowed them to preempt his attacks and cut off his supply lines. Despite the fact the world was still unaware of Che's whereabouts, the U.S. government was well aware of his locations and activities: The National Security Agency (NSA) was

GUEVARA THE POET

Che Guevara, a prolific author, wrote more than just books on guerrilla warfare, political theory, and his revolutionary adventures. A lover of poetry, the rebel leader himself wrote poems. The following is a poem he wrote for his wife Aleida toward the end of the failed Bolivian expedition. It is written in the form of a last will and testament and is entitled "Against Wind and Tide."

This poem (against wind and tide) will carry my signature.
I give to you six sonorous syllables
a look which always bears (like a wounded bird) tenderness,

An anxiety of lukewarm deep water,
a dark office where the only light is these verses of mine
a very used thimble for your bored nights,
a photograph of our sons.

The most beautiful bullet in this pistol that always accompanies me,
the unerasable memory (always latent and deep) of the children
who, one day, you and I conceived,
and the piece of life that remains for me,

This I give (convinced and happy) to the Revolution.
Nothing that can unite us will have greater power.

Jon Lee Anderson, *Che: A Revolutionary Life*. New York: Grove Press, 1997, p. 730.

Che Guevara holds a Congolese boy and stands next to a local guerrilla. In 1965, after he left Cuba, Che went to the Congo to help support the Marxist Simba movement.

intercepting all of his incoming and outgoing communications via equipment aboard the USNS *Pvt Jose F. Valdez* (T-AG-169), a floating listening post that cruised the Indian Ocean near Dar es Salaam, Tanzania.

Che's goal was to export the Cuban Revolution to the Congo by instructing the local Simba fighters in Marxist ideology and strategies of "foco" theory of guerrilla warfare. Che introduced the foco theory of revolutionary warfare to the world in his book *Guerrilla Warfare*, in which he insists that a small group of dedicated men can create the conditions of a revolution and set it off as well. Although this theory stands in opposition to traditional Marxist theory, which states that revolutionary conditions must naturally develop within a society for a revolution to be successful, Che was there to oversee its success.

Che was unable to achieve his goal, however. In his Congo diary, Che cites incompetence, stubbornness, and infighting by the local Congolese forces as reasons for the revolt's failure. In truth, the revolt also failed in part because Che himself was failing. Suffering from dysentery and his usual acute asthma, Guevara was not at his best either physically or mentally.

After seven months in the Congo, a disheartened Che left with the Cuban survivors. (Six members of his column had died.) At one point Guevara considered sending the wounded back to Cuba while continuing to fight alone in the Congo until his death, thus providing the world a model of a true revolutionary in action willing to die for a cause. But urged by his comrades and pressed by two emissaries from Castro, at the last moment he agreed to retreat. A few weeks later, he sat down to write the preface for the diary he had kept during his time in the Congo. He began, "This is the history of a failure."

Guevara was reluctant to return to Cuba, if only because Castro had made public Guevara's "farewell letter," a letter he had written to Castro meant to be revealed to the world only in the case of his death. In the letter, Che cut himself from all

A COMPLICATED LEGACY

With Che Guevara, as with other recent controversial historical figures, history's final judgment, his legacy, is still to be determined.

To some, he is the ideal rebel, a man who gave his life so that others might enjoy freedom and equality. Nelson Mandela, for one, has called him "an inspiration for every human being who loves freedom." To others, he is a brilliant philosopher and teacher on how to fight and win a guerrilla war. Others see him as a man who tossed aside his own comfortable life to stand firmly on the side of those in need. Of course, others see him as nothing more than a mass murderer, interested in nothing but power for power's sake, a man whose goal was to avenge with blood those whom he deemed the enemy. In other words, they see him as nothing more than a terrorist.

Judging Che is, to say the least, somewhat confusing—but then, very few people are all good or all evil. Most heroes have their flaws; most people called "evil" have their positive attributes as well. Perhaps the most important part of Che's legacy to date is the image he has presented to young people worldwide, a representation of the ideal of fighting for a common cause, for rebelling against the "powers that be" and standing up for what is right.

Consider this: In the spring of 1999, the rector of Mexico City's UNAM (National Autonomous University of Mexico) decided to raise student tuitions by 3,000 percent. When student leaders met to organize mass protests and student strikes against the tuition hike, they met in the school's auditorium—the Che Guevara auditorium.

ties with Cuba, resigning his positions in the party, as minister, as commander—even his Cuban citizenship.

He had gone on in his farewell letter thanking the Cuban people for everything they had given him, for allowing him to be a part of their revolution, and vowing to continue the fight worldwide, no matter the personal cost.

I carry to new battlefronts the faith that you taught me, the revolutionary spirit of my people, the feeling of fulfilling the most sacred of duties: to fight against imperialism where it might be. This is a source of strength, and more than heals the deepest of wounds...

If my final hour finds me under other skies, my last thought will be of this people and especially of you [Fidel Castro]. I am grateful for your teaching and your example, to which I shall try to be faithful up to the final consequences of my acts.[3]

For the next six months, Guevara lived, unknown to the rest of the world, in Dar es Salaam. During this time, he compiled his memories of the Congo experience and wrote drafts of two more books, one on philosophy and the other on economics. He then visited several Western European countries to test his new false identity papers, created by Cuban Intelligence for his later travels to South America. After stopping in Cuba to train his troops and briefly visit his family, on November 3, 1966, Che left for Bolivia. It would be his last revolutionary adventure.

BOLIVIA AND DEATH

Just 11 months later, his dream of revolution in Bolivia, one of Latin America's poorest nations—of creating a rebel army capable of overthrowing the U.S. supported government of President Rene Barrientos Ortuño—had ended in utter failure. Régis Debray, a French intellectual who was captured in April 1967 while with Guevara, described the desperate conditions in which the rebels found themselves living during their last months there. But despite suffering from malnutrition, lack of water, lack of shoes, and possessing only six blankets for 22 men, Guevara still remained optimistic about the future of Latin America. His belief in the power of change was unshakeable.

Che was captured by Bolivian Special Forces on October 7, 1967, and two days later was summarily executed by order of

A boy holds a poster of Che Guevara in Vallegrande, Bolivia, in 2006, nearly 40 years after the revolutionary's death. Today, Che's face symbolizes different things to different people, but there is no denying the mark he made on history.

President Barrientos. On October 15, Castro announced to the Cuban people that Guevara was dead and proclaimed three days of public mourning throughout the island.

On October 18, Castro addressed a crowd estimated at almost one million people in Havana and spoke about Guevara's character as a revolutionary, telling the grieving Cuban people:

If we want the . . . model of a human being who does not belong to our time but to the future, I say from the depth of my heart that such a model, without a single stain on his conduct, without a single stain on his behavior, is Che! If we wish to express what we want our children to be, we must say from our very hearts as ardent revolutionaries: we want them to be like Che![4]

For years, the resting place of Guevera's remains was unknown. But in late 1995, retired Bolivian general Mario Vargas revealed to Jon Lee Anderson, author of *Che Guevara: A Revolutionary Life*, that his body had been buried near a Vallegrande airstrip. In July 1997, a team of Cuban geologists and Argentine forensic anthropologists discovered the remnants of seven bodies in two mass graves, including one man with amputated hands (like Guevara). Officials with Bolivia's Ministry of Interior later identified the body as Guevara when the excavated teeth proved to be a perfect match of a plaster mold of Che's teeth made in Cuba shortly before the beginning of his Congolese expedition.

On October 17, 1997, Guevara's remains, along with those of his six fellow fighters, were laid to rest with full military honors in a specially built mausoleum in the city of Santa Clara, the city where Che had won the decisive military victory of the Cuban Revolution. With that, the body of Ernesto Che Guevara, who had traveled the world in search of adventure and revolution, arrived at its final resting place.

In many ways, Che Guevara never died. His image looks out at us from T-shirts, from posters, from magazine covers. If anything, as biographer Jorge Castañeda points out, it was his death that gave meaning to his life. Because he died, because he was executed in the cause of revolution, because he gave his life in the cause of helping others, he became a martyr and symbol of revolution.

All around the world, wherever young people are marching, wherever miners are standing up for the right to fair working conditions, wherever peasants call out for reform, the spirit of Che Guevara is there. As Chilean dissident and author Ariel Dorfman wrote in his 1999 essay on Guevara:

> Even though I have come to be wary of dead heroes and the overwhelming burden their martyrdom imposes on the living, I will allow myself a prophecy. Or maybe it is a warning. More than 3 billion human beings on this planet right now live on less than $2 a day. And every day that breaks, 40,000 children—more than one every second!—succumb to diseases linked to chronic hunger. They are there, always there, the terrifying conditions of injustice and inequality that led Che many decades ago to start his journey toward that bullet and that photo awaiting him in Bolivia. The powerful of the earth should take heed: deep inside that T shirt where we have tried to trap him, the eyes of Che Guevara are still burning with impatience.[5]

Though he is seen by some as a killer who has been romanticized over time, by devoting himself to the cause of revolution, Ernesto "Che" Guevara made himself a hero to millions and an inspiration to some who also want to give of themselves for the betterment of others.

Chronology

1928   Ernesto Guevara is born on June 14, the first child of Ernesto Guevara Lynch and Celia de la Serna.

1932   The Guevara family moves from Buenos Aires to Alta Gracia in an attempt to find a climate that might help ease Che's chronic asthma.

1948   Abandoning his initial plan to study engineering, Che enrolls in medical school at the University of Buenos Aires. While there, he holds down a series of part-time jobs, including one at an allergy clinic.

1952   Guevara and his friend Alberto Granado travel throughout South America, initially on motorcycle, then by other means of transportation. Che's travels will be immortalized in the journal of his travels, published as *The Motorcycle Diaries*.

1953   Guevara graduates from medical school and quickly leaves on another trip around Latin America, visiting Bolivia, Peru, Ecuador, Panama, Costa Rica, and Guatemala.

1954   Guevara's political beliefs become radicalized in Guatemala, where he witnesses the overthrow of the democratically elected government by U.S.-backed forces. He escapes to Mexico, where he marries Peruvian Hilda Gadea, with whom he has a daughter, Hildita.

1955   After meeting Fidel Castro, Guevara decides to join the group being organized to wage guerrilla war against the Batista government in Cuba.

1956–1958   In November 1956, Che arrives in Cuba as the troops' doctor, but quickly falls into a military role. Demonstrating outstanding military ability, he is promoted to the rank of *Commandante* in July 1957. In December 1958 he leads the rebel army to a decisive victory over the Cuban army at Santa Clara.

1959   Che is declared a citizen of Cuba in recognition of his contribution to the island's liberation. He divorces Hilda Gadea and marries Aleida March,

with whom he has four children. He assumes several
governmental positions, including commander of
the La Cabana Fortress prison, head of the Industrial
Department of the Institute of Agrarian Reform, and
president of the National Bank of Cuba. In a sign of
his contempt for money, he signs the new banknotes
simply as "Che."

1960   Che leaves Cuba for an extensive diplomatic tour of
the Soviet Union, East Germany, Japan, and China,
among other countries.

1961   Che is appointed head of the newly established
Ministry of Industry.

1962   Che is the guiding force in the decision to allow the
Soviet Union to install nuclear missiles in Cuba. After
the Cuban Missile Crisis, the missiles are removed,
leading Che to question his nation's relationship with
the Soviet Union.

1928
Ernesto Guevara is
born on June 14

1953
Graduates from
medical school and
travels to Bolivia,
Peru, Ecuador,
Panama, Costa Rica,
and Guatemala

1955
Meets Fidel Castro and
joins the group being
organized to wage
guerrilla war against
the Batista government
in Cuba

1928   1958

1952
Travels with Alberto
Granado throughout
South America

1954
Marries Peruvian
Hilda Gadea, with
whom he has a
daughter, Hildita

1958
Leads the rebel
army to a decisive
victory over the
Cuban army at
Santa Clara

1964–1965 Che addresses the United Nations in December 1964 and ends his speech with a stirring recitation of the *Second Declaration of Havana*. After leaving New York, Guevara begins a three-month world tour. In Algiers, Guevara gives a speech attacking the Soviet Union and other Eastern Bloc nations as his Marxist sympathies shift toward Mao Zedong and the People's Republic of China.

1965 Returning to Cuba in March 1965, Che disappears from public view. He ends up in the Congo, where he hopes to lead a liberation movement against the government. While there, Castro reads Che's farewell letter to Cuba, wherein he resigned all government positions and gave up his Cuban citizenship in favor of assisting revolutionary movements worldwide.

1966 After the Congo mission ends in failure, Che arrives disguised in Bolivia.

1959
Divorces Hilda Gadea and marries Aleida March, with whom he has four children

1962
Che is the guiding force in the decision to allow the Soviet Union to install nuclear missiles in Cuba

1965
In the Congo, begins a liberation movement against the government

1959

1967

1960
Embarks on a diplomatic tour of the Soviet Union, East Germany, Japan, and China

1964
Addresses the United Nations and ends his speech with a stirring recitation of the *Second Declaration of Havana*

1967
On October 8, Che is wounded and captured by Bolivian forces assisted by the CIA. He is murdered the following day

1967   On October 8, Che is wounded and captured by Bolivian forces assisted by the CIA. He is murdered the following day.

1997   Che Guevara's remains are located in Bolivia and returned to Cuba, where they are placed in a memorial at Santa Clara.

Notes

Chapter 1

1 "Castro's Brain," *Time*, August 8, 1960. http://www.time.com/time/magazine/article/0,9171,869742,00.html.

2 Jon Lee Anderson, *Che: A Revolutionary Life*. New York: Grove Press, 1997, p. 733.

3 Anderson, p. 737.

4 Michele Ray, "In Cold Blood: The Execution of Che by the CIA," *Ramparts*, March 1968.

5 Anderson, p. 739.

6 Jorge G. Castañeda, *Compañero: the Life and Death of Che Guevara*. New York: Vintage Books, 1998, p. xiv.

7 Ariel Dorfman, "Che Guevara: The *Time* 100," *Time*, June 14, 1999. www.time.com/time/time100/heroes/profile/guevara01.html.

8 Anderson, p. xiii.

9 Anderson, p. 465.

10 Paul Vallely, "Che Guevara: When the Reality Becomes Myth," *Independent*, August 28, 2004. http://www.independent.co.uk/news/people/profiles/che-guevara-when-the-reality-becomes-myth-558047.html.

11 Dorfman, "Che Guevara: The *Time* 100."

12 *Shorter Oxford English Dictionary*. New York: Oxford University Press, 2002, p. 2569.

13 *Shorter Oxford English Dictionary*, p. 2568.

14 Paul Berman, "The Cult of Che: Don't Applaud *The Motorcycle Diaries*," *Slate*, September 24, 2004. http://www.slate.com/id/2107100/.

Chapter 2

1 Castañeda, p. 11.

2 Ibid.

3 Anderson, p. 19.

4 Castañeda, p. 13.

5 Castañeda, p. 14.

6 Castañeda, p. 15.

7 Castañeda, p. 19.

8 Castañeda, pp. 20–21.

9 Anderson, p. 36.

10 Ibid.

11 Castañeda, pp. 22–23.

Chapter 3

1 Anderson, p. 41.

2 Anderson, p. 42.

3 Ernesto Che Guevara, *The Motorcycle Diaries: Notes on a Latin American Journey*. New York: Ocean Press, 2003, pp. 53–54.

4 Guevara, *The Motorcycle Diaries*, p. 70.

5 Guevara, *The Motorcycle Diaries*, pp. 77–78.

6 Anderson, p. 80.

7 Anderson, p. 82.

8 Anderson, p. 84.

9 Ibid.

10 Anderson, p. 85.

11 Castañeda, p. 52.

12 Ibid..

13 Castañeda, p. 52.

Chapter 4

1 Guevara, *The Motorcycle Diaries*, p. 32.

2 Anderson, p. 97.

3 Ibid.

4 Anderson, p. 98.

5 Castañeda, p. 57.

6 Castañeda, p. 59.

7 Ibid.

8 Ernesto Guevara Lynch, *Aqui Va un Soldado de America*. Barcelona: Plaza y Janes Editores, S.A., 2000, p. 26.

9 Andrew Sinclair, *Che Guevara*. New York: Viking Press, 1970, p. 12.

10 Castañeda, p. 76.

11 Castañeda, p. 77.

Chapter 5

1 Castañeda, p. 80.
2 Castañeda, p. 83.
3 David Sandison, *The Life and Times of Che Guevara.* New York: Parragon Book Service, 1996, p. 28.
4 Castañeda, p. 84.
5 Anderson, p. 194.
6 Castañeda, p. 94.
7 Anderson, p. 207.
8 Anthony DePalma, *The Man Who Invented Fidel: Castro, Cuba, and Herbert L. Matthews of the New York Times.* New York: Public Affairs, 2006, p. 103.
9 "Castro's Brain," *Time.*
10 Anderson, p. 237.
11 Ignacio Ramonet, *Fidel Castro: My Life*, trans. by Andrew Hurley. London: Penguin Books, 2007, p. 177.
12 Anderson, p. 242.
13 Anderson, p. 243.
14 Anderson, p. 245.

Chapter 6

1 Castañeda, p. 104.
2 Castañeda, p. 108.
3 Castañeda, p. 122.
4 USMC Major Larry James Bockman, *The Spirit of Moncada: Fidel Castro's Rise to Power, 1953–1959.* United States: Marine Corp Command and Staff College, April 1, 1984.
5 Department of State Cable, "Ambassador Report on Meeting with Castro," September 4, 1959. http://www.swl.net/patepluma/central/cuba/rebel2.html.
6 Castañeda, p. 137.
7 Castañeda, p. 141.
8 Anderson, p. 390.
9 Anderson, p. 375.
10 Castañeda, p. 150.

11 Castañeda, p. 166.
12 Anderson, p. 435.
13 Castañeda, p. 169.
14 Che Guevara, "Socialism and man in Cuba," March 12, 1965. www.marxist.org/archive/guevara/1965/03/man-socialism.htm.

Chapter 7

1 Anderson, p. 416.
2 Department of State Cable, "Ambassador Report on Meeting with Castro."
3 Anderson, p. 392.
4 Anderson, p. 509.
5 Anderson, p. 508.
6 Anderson, p. 530.
7 Castañeda, p. 231.
8 Castañeda, p. 178.
9 Che Guevara, "At the United Nations," December 11, 1964. www.marxists.org/archive/guevara/1964/12/11.htm.
10 Ibid.
11 Ibid.
12 Ibid.
13 Ibid.
14 Ibid.
15 Ibid.
16 Ibid.
17 Ibid.
18 Ibid.
19 Guevera, "Socialism and Man in Cuba."

Chapter 8

1 Castañeda, pp. 303–304.
2 Anderson, p. 623.
3 Ernesto Che Guevara, "Farewell Letter from Che to Fidel Castro," April 1, 1965. www.marxist.org/archive/guevara/1965/04/01.htm.
4 Anderson, p. 741.
5 Dorfman, "Che Guevara: The *Time* 100."

Bibliography

Anderson, Jon Lee. *Che: A Revolutionary Life*. New York: Grove Press, 1997.

Berman, Paul. "The Cult of Che: Don't Applaud *The Motorcycle Diaries*." *Slate*. Available online. URL: http://www.slate.com/id/2107100/. September 24, 2004.

Bockman, USMC Major Larry James. *The Spirit of Moncada: Fidel Castro's Rise to Power, 1953–1959*. United States: Marine Corp Command and Staff College. April 1, 1984.

Casey, Michael. *Che's Afterlife: The Legacy of an Image*. New York: Vintage Books, 2009.

Castañeda, Jorge G. *Compañero: The Life and Death of Che Guevara*. New York: Vintage Books, 1998.

"Castro's Brain." *Time*. Available online. URL: http://www.time.com/time/magazine/article/0.971,869742,00.html. August 8, 1960.

"Che: A Myth Embalmed in a Matrix of Ignorance." *Time*. Available online. URL: http://www.time.com/time/magazine/article/0,9171,942333,00.html. October 12, 1970.

DePalma, Anthony. *The Man Who Invented Fidel: Castro, Cuba, and Herbert L. Matthews of the New York Times*. New York: Public Affairs, 2006.

Department of State Cable. "Ambassador Report on Meeting with Castro." September 4, 1959. Available online. URL: http://www.swl.net/patepluma/central/cuba/rebel2.html.

Dorfman, Ariel. "Che Guevara: The *Time* 100." *Time*. Available online. URL: www.time.com/time/time100/heroes/profile/guevara01.html. June 14, 1999.

Guevara, Che. "At the United Nations." Speech before 19th General Assembly of the United Nations in New York. Available online. URL: www.marxists.org/archive/guevara/1964/12/11.htm. December 11, 1964.

Guevara, Che. "Socialism and Man in Cuba." Available online. URL: www.marxists.org/archive/guevara/1965/03/man-socialism.htm. March 12, 1965.

Guevara, Ernesto Che. "Farewell Letter from Che to Fidel Castro." Available online. URL: www.marxists.org/archive/guevara/1965/04/01.htm. April 1, 1965.

Guevara, Ernesto Che. *The Motorcycle Diaries: Notes on a Latin American Journey*. New York: Ocean Press, 2003.

Guevara Lynch, Ernesto. *Aqui Va un Soldado de America*. Barcelona: Plaza y Janes Editores, S.A., 2000.

Ramonet, Ignacio. *Fidel Castro: My Life*. Translated by Andrew Hurley. London: Penguin Books, 2007.

Ray, Michele. "In Cold Blood: The Execution of Che by the CIA." *Ramparts*, March 1968.

Sandison, David. *The Life and Times of Che Guevara*. New York: Parragon Book Service, 1996.

Shorter Oxford English Dictionary. New York: Oxford University Press, 2002.

Tamayo, Juan O. "The Man Who Buried Che." Available online. URL: www.fiu.edu/~fcf/cheremains111897.html. September 19, 1997.

Vallely, Paul. "Che Guevara: When the Reality Becomes Myth." *Independent*. Available online. URL: http://www.independent.co.uk/news/people/profiles/che-guevara-when-the-reality-becomes-myth-558047.html. August 28, 2004.

Further Reading

Balfour, Sebastian. *Castro*, 2nd ed. New York: Longman, 2003.

Fontova, Humberto. *Exposing the Real Che Guevara and the Useful Idiots Who Idolize Him*. New York: Sentinel Trade, 2008.

Galeano, Eduardo. *Open Veins of Latin America: Five Centuries of the Pillage of a Continent*. Monthly Review Press, 1997.

Guevara, Ernesto Che. *Che Guevara Talks to Young People*. Atlanta, Ga.: Pathfinder, 2000.

Guevara, Ernesto Che. *Reminiscences of the Cuban Revolutionary War: Authorized Edition*. New York: Ocean Press, 2005.

Picture Credits

Index

About the Author

Dennis Abrams is the author of numerous books for Chelsea House, including biographies of Barbara Park, Nicolas Sarkozy, Rachael Ray, Georgia O'Keeffe, Albert Pujols, Jay-Z, and Xerxes the Great. He attended Antioch College, where he majored in English and communications. A voracious reader since the age of three, Dennis lives in Houston, Texas, with his partner of 20 years, along with their two cats and their dog, Junie B.